D1556987

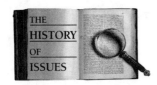

THE
HISTORY
OF
ISSUES

Military Draft

Other Books in the History of Issues Series:

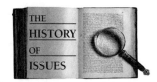

THE
HISTORY
OF
ISSUES

Military Draft

Jeff Hay, Book Editor

GREENHAVEN PRESS

An imprint of Thomson Gale, a part of The Thomson Corporation

Detroit • New York • San Francisco • New Haven, Conn. • Waterville, Maine • London

Christine Nasso, *Publisher*
Elizabeth Des Chenes, *Managing Editor*

For more information, contact:
Greenhaven Press
27500 Drake Rd.
Farmington Hills, MI 48331-3535
Or you can visit our Internet site at http://www.gale.com

LIBRARY OF CONGRESS CATALOGING-IN-PUBLICATION DATA

Military draft / Jeff Hay, book editor.
  p. cm. -- (History of issues)
  Includes bibliographical references and index.
  ISBN-13: 978-0-7377-3842-1 (hbk.)
  1. Draft--United States. 2. Draft--History. I. Hay, Jeff, 1964-
  UB323.M536 2008
  355.2'23630973--dc22

2007029821

ISBN-10: 0-7377-3842-1 (hbk.)

Printed in the United States of America
10 9 8 7 6 5 4 3 2 1

Contents

Chapter 1: The Military Draft from the French Revolution Through World War II

Chapter 2: The Notion of National Service and the Military Needs of the Cold War

Chapter 4: The Military Draft in Recent Times

Foreword

In the 1940s, at the height of the Holocaust, Jews struggled to create a nation of their own in Palestine, a region of the Middle East that at the time was controlled by Britain. The British had placed limits on Jewish immigration to Palestine, hampering efforts to provide refuge to Jews fleeing the Holocaust. In response to this and other British policies, an underground Jewish resistance group called Irgun began carrying out terrorist attacks against British targets in Palestine, including immigration, intelligence, and police offices. Most famously, the group bombed the King David Hotel in Jerusalem, the site of a British military headquarters. Although the British were warned well in advance of the attack, they failed to evacuate the building. As a result, ninety-one people were killed (including fifteen Jews) and forty-five were injured.

Early in the twentieth century, Ireland, which had long been under British rule, was split into two countries. The south, populated mostly by Catholics, eventually achieved independence and became the Republic of Ireland. Northern Ireland, mostly Protestant, remained under British control. Catholics in both the north and south opposed British control of the north, and the Irish Republican Army (IRA) sought unification of Ireland as an independent nation. In 1969, the IRA split into two factions. A new radical wing, the Provisional IRA, was created and soon undertook numerous terrorist bombings and killings throughout Northern Ireland, the Republic of Ireland, and even in England. One of its most notorious attacks was the 1974 bombing of a Birmingham, England, bar that killed nineteen people.

In the mid-1990s, an Islamic terrorist group called al Qaeda began carrying out terrorist attacks against American targets overseas. In communications to the media, the organization listed several complaints against the United States. It generally opposed all U.S. involvement and presence in the Middle East. It particularly objected to the presence of U.S. troops in Saudi Arabia, which is the home of several Islamic holy sites. And it strongly condemned the United States for supporting the nation of Israel, which it claimed was an oppressor of Muslims. In 1998 al Qaeda's leaders issued a fatwa (a religious legal statement) calling for Muslims to kill Americans. Al Qaeda acted on this order many times—most memorably on September 11, 2001, when it attacked the World Trade Center and the Pentagon, killing nearly three thousand people.

These three groups—Irgun, the Provisional IRA, and al Qaeda—have achieved varied results. Irgun's terror campaign contributed to Britain's decision to pull out of Palestine and to support the creation of Israel in 1948. The Provisional IRA's tactics kept pressure on the British, but they also alienated many would-be supporters of independence for Northern Ireland. Al Qaeda's attacks provoked a strong U.S. military response but did not lessen America's involvement in the Middle East nor weaken its support of Israel. Despite these different results, the means and goals of these groups were similar. Although they emerged in different parts of the world during different eras and in support of different causes, all three had one thing in common: They all used clandestine violence to undermine a government they deemed oppressive or illegitimate.

The destruction of oppressive governments is not the only goal of terrorism. For example, terror is also used to minimize dissent in totalitarian regimes and to promote extreme ideologies. However, throughout history the motivations of terrorists have been remarkably similar, proving the old adage that "the more things change, the more they remain the same." Arguments for and against terrorism thus boil down to the same set of universal arguments regardless of the age: Some argue that terrorism is justified to change (or, in the case of state terror, to maintain) the prevailing political order; others respond that terrorism is inhumane and unacceptable under any circumstances. These basic views transcend time and place.

Similar fundamental arguments apply to other controversial social issues. For instance, arguments over the death penalty have always featured competing views of justice. Scholars cite biblical texts to claim that a person who takes a life must forfeit his or her life, while others cite religious doctrine to support their view that only God can take a human life. These arguments have remained essentially the same throughout the centuries. Likewise, the debate over euthanasia has persisted throughout the history of Western civilization. Supporters argue that it is compassionate to end the suffering of the dying by hastening their impending death; opponents insist that it is society's duty to make the dying as comfortable as possible as death takes its natural course.

Greenhaven Press's The History of Issues series illustrates this constancy of arguments surrounding major social issues. Each volume in the series focuses on one issue—including terrorism, the death penalty, and euthanasia—and examines how the debates have both evolved and remained essentially the same over the years. Primary documents such as newspaper articles, speeches, and government reports illuminate historical developments and offer perspectives from throughout history. Secondary sources provide overviews and commentaries from a more contemporary perspective. An introduction begins each anthology and supplies essential context and background. An annotated table of contents, chronology, and index allow for easy reference, and a bibliography and list of organizations to contact point to additional sources of information on the book's topic. With these features, The History of Issues series permits readers to glimpse both the historical and contemporary dimensions of humanity's most pressing and controversial social issues.

Introduction

During Bill Clinton's first campaign for the presidency in 1992, and even during his eight years in office, critics wondered whether he had enough credibility with the military to serve as its commander in chief in the event of war. They claimed that he had been a draft-dodger as a young man. Indeed, Clinton did not serve in the armed forces during the Vietnam War years of the 1960s and early 1970s, when millions of men of his generation were drafted into service. Instead, he was a university student during the years when he was most likely to have been called up. Like millions of others, Clinton was able to avoid being drafted by going to a university. The draft laws then in place allowed for that.

The Vietnam War draft forced young men into making difficult choices, and in so doing it illustrated the struggle that lies at the heart of almost all modern draft laws and the controversies that they inspire: the conflict between the obligations of citizenship and the right to personal freedom that might be infringed upon by being required to serve. Some argue that military service is similar to paying taxes or obeying laws; it is one of the duties one owes to the nation where one lives. Others argue that requiring military service is a form of involuntary servitude, even slavery, and that such requirements are unreasonable in free nations.

Bill Clinton was not strictly speaking a draft-dodger. He was never drafted in the first place thanks to the deferments and exemptions available to him. Others such as George W. Bush, avoided the dangers of the Vietnam War by serving in the National Guard at home. Still others sought to preempt the draft by volunteering, thus making themselves eligible for relatively safe military duty. Still others, such as the famous boxer Muhammad Ali (then known as Cassius Clay), went to prison rather than accept a draft. The Vietnam War draft, like virtually all drafts in the last two hundred or more years, inspired this wide range of responses, and any new draft would likely do the same.

The First National Army

The first modern draft was enacted in France during the years of the French Revolution (1789–1815). Then, partly following the model already set by America's thirteen colonies, French reformers sought to create a state based upon individual freedoms and the rights of man. Europe's monarchs, fearful of the spread of this "revolutionary" ideology, went to war with France to try to contain it, as well as, hopefully, reestablish the absolute power that France's kings and nobles had enjoyed before. To ensure that they had enough soldiers to defend the nation against these threats, France's leaders enacted a *levée en masse* in 1793. This mass conscription called upon all who were able to serve France militarily, while other calls went out for older men, women, and indeed anyone who could make uniforms or gunpowder, staff offices, or do anything at all that might help in the national defense. Many Frenchmen resisted this initial call, although later draft laws allowed France to build a *grande armée* that, under Napoleon in the early 1800s, conquered much of Europe.

Another European nation, Prussia, enacted its own mass conscription in 1813. Prussia, which in the 1860s and 1870s led the process which resulted in a unified Germany, was the first country to continue with the practice of conscription over a period of many decades. In the United States, meanwhile, the War of 1812 against Great Britain spurred calls for a draft, but they were spurned by the U.S. Congress. The prominent statesman Daniel Webster made a speech against this proposed draft in 1814. In it, he asked "where is it written in the Constitution . . . that you may take children from their parents, and parents from their children, and compel them to fight the battles of any war, in which the folly or wickedness

15

of Government may engage it?" Webster thought that the Constitution's provisions for raising citizen's militias for the defense of the country (not for foreign wars) were more than enough. Any further conscription, for him, amounted to tyranny.

America's First Draft Law Inspires Riots

During the American Civil War of 1861 to 1865, both sides enacted a draft. The law adopted by the northern Union was especially contentious, and it made clear another of the problems of modern draft laws: who had to serve, and who might be exempt. The Union's law required communities which had failed to provide enough troops through voluntary means to draft the remainder. However, those drafted could provide substitutes or pay three hundred dollars for an exemption. Unsurprisingly, most of those who could afford the exemption paid the three hundred dollars, meaning that in effect, the rich were exempted from the draft. These inequities helped to inspire antidraft riots that swept New York and other cities in 1863. In the end, only 2 percent of the troops who fought for the Union were draftees, and in December 1864 the draft law expired and was not renewed.

By the early twentieth century the nature of warfare had changed and, along with it, thinking about the draft. World War I, the first major conflict of the century, fought from 1914 to 1918, was a "total" war. In such a conflict, armies were so big and weapons so powerful that most of the resources of nations had to be devoted to the war effort. Most of the millions of troops who fought in World War I's trenches were draftees who believed they were doing their duty. This was even true for Great Britain, a nation which had traditionally avoided conscription both because it relied on a large navy rather than a standing army and because of its custom of respecting individual liberty. Meanwhile, even citizens who did not serve in uniform were expected to work in munitions factories or in some other behind-the-lines capacity.

The conscription practices of World War I were certainly based on military necessity, but they were partly justified on the grounds that citizens should be expected to perform some sort of national service, whether in uniform or civilian clothes. Of course, it was only governments that had the ability to organize and manage these various national service programs, meaning that governments' ability to make demands on ordinary people would increase. Such thinking was a marked contrast from that of Daniel Webster a century earlier. Instead of considering a draft "tyranny," many people in the early twentieth century thought that governments had a fundamental right to demand time and service from their citizens.

Universal Military Training

This sort of thinking was most common in Europe and Japan, but it also appeared in the United States. The so-called Plattsburg movement, begun in 1914, sought to train citizen-soldiers outside of the military's regular procedures, a fledgling attempt to introduce universal military training (UMT) into the United States. And when the United States entered World War I in 1917, a new draft was enacted. It required all men ages twenty-one to thirty-five to register for selective service, with a later version of the law extending the age range from eighteen to forty-five. A few people, among them ministers and students of the ministry, were exempt.

The 1917 draft law inspired much debate. Arizona congressman Carl Hayden was "convinced that most of the propaganda in favor of selected conscription is founded not so much upon a desire to win the war as it is to accustom the people to this method of raising armies and thereby to establish it as a permanent system in this country." He also referred to it as an echo of the "Prussian militarism" that the U.S. effort in World War I was to oppose. Even after it was enacted, the draft continued to garner much opposition, both active and passive. During the first round of call-ups, 50 percent of those called asked for exemptions, while tens of thousands of draftees chose not to show up at all (and were not arrested). As the draft continued many people left the country to avoid the draft, or even had teeth pulled so that they would not meet the physical requirements.

In an era of nearly universal drafts, an inevitable question arose: what to do with conscientious objectors (COs), or those who rejected violence on religious grounds. Should they still be expected to serve? At the heart of this question was the extent to which governments had the right to impinge upon deeply held religious or ethical beliefs. During World War I, COs were indeed called up. But they were exempted from combat duty provided they could prove conclusively the depths of their beliefs. This usually meant demonstrating that they were active members of pacifist religious groups like the Quakers.

After World War I the American draft ended, although calls continued to be heard from "Plattsburgers" and others for universal military training. Meanwhile, international tensions, and fears of a future large-scale war, mounted. The new communist regime in the Russian Empire, the Soviet Union, made conscription in both military or labor service compulsory for both men and women by 1930. The fascist regimes in Italy and Germany also introduced a universal draft which also, eventually, included labor service for women. These regimes, admittedly, cared little for the principle of personal freedom; service to the state and its ideology was paramount. In the United States, meanwhile, leaders enacted a Selective Service Committee in 1926. Among its tasks was to prepare manpower estimates for future wars and, along with them, rough drafts of new draft bills.

Germany led Europe into World War II in 1939, and Japan soon extended its war in China to conflicts in Southeast Asia.

World War II was another total war requiring contributions from almost all citizens, from industry, and from all important resources. Struggling to survive the German onslaught, Great Britain in May 1940 adopted a law that allowed the government to draft whatever resources necessary, including people. While men were generally filtered into the armed services, unmarried British women under thirty were required to register for labor service, a striking development in a nation with Britain's tradition of individual liberty.

America's First Peacetime Draft

America's selective service machinery, under preparation since 1926, started full operation in the fall of 1940. Then, America's first-ever peacetime draft was enacted. It required men from ages twenty-one to thirty-five to register, with the possibility that they might be drafted for a year's service. As in the War of 1812 and World War I, congressional debate over the draft was blunt and outspoken, with many politicians comparing it to the operations of a dictatorship. Congressman Frank Keefe of Wisconsin voiced a further concern: that a draft might give the military too much power over the lives of its citizens. He was concerned that "this control may be exercised through the allocation of men to particular industries as a condition of continued deferment, and compels millions of others, regardless of will, to be subjected to conscription at any time." Indeed, objections were strong enough that the draft bill passed only narrowly, and was to be in force for only one year.

Admittedly much of the opposition in Congress to the 1940 draft bill was based on the concern that it would lead the United States into World War II, a development many hoped could be prevented. But by late 1941, German submarines were attacking American ships in the Atlantic Ocean and, on December 7 of that year, Japan bombarded the American naval base at Pearl Harbor in Hawaii. America was now in the war. Not only was the 1940 law renewed and broadened, opposition to it became increasingly muted. By war's end in 1945, some ten million Americans were drafted, and they remained in service for the duration of the conflict rather than for a single year. Although most young men had to register for the draft, some deferments were possible. University students in science and engineering fields were able to put off being drafted, while some draftees were even sent to colleges to receive the sorts of training military authorities deemed desirable prior to active duty. Meanwhile legislation also provided exemptions for conscientious objectors provided they performed some sort of useful civilian work. Those who refused to register or to go when they were called up were sometimes imprisoned.

The World War II selective service law expired in March 1947 and was not immediately renewed by the U.S. Congress. Indeed, some members of Congress, as well as civilian organizations, tried in this period to outlaw further conscription measures in peacetime. They feared that not only would a draft violate rights to individual freedom, but also that the presence of a large standing army might encourage the president to use it in overseas military adventures not approved by Congress.

These objections were unable to prevent the establishment of a new draft. In the late 1940s the Cold War was taking shape. This was a long conflict of threats and escalating tensions between the United States and its allies, on the one hand, and the Communist Soviet Union and its allies on the other. The center of the Cold War was Europe, half of which was already under Soviet influence by the end of World War II. American political and military leaders wanted to make sure that they had enough manpower in the event of a land war in Europe against the Soviets, thus, in June 1948, the draft was reinstituted. This particular draft law was continually renewed (often with variations) until it expired in 1973.

Most of America's allies in Western Europe also maintained forms of conscription as the Cold War took shape. Commonly, nations required periods of military training for young men, generally of less than a year. Afterward most of these trainees were considered members of military reserves. Indeed, military training became an expected rite of passage for many young men in continental Europe, and it remains so today in such nations as Sweden, Norway, and Switzerland. Even Great Britain, a nation that had traditionally only drafted people in times of war, maintained a program of "national service" from 1947 to 1963.

Draft proposals in this era sometimes went beyond calls for military training. In America there were renewed calls from some quarters for not only universal military training (UMT), but for mandatory national service as well. These proposals suggested that young Americans might serve in ways beyond the military, such as in educational corps or other civic organizations. Proponents argued that such programs might enhance the social and work skills of participants as well as encourage patriotism. They might also involve young women, the first time in the American experience that the "drafting" of women was considered. But, despite the support these proposals received from such leaders as Dwight D. Eisenhower—a World War II general and president from 1953 to 1961—they were never seriously considered by Congress.

Opposing the Draft in the Vietnam Era

In 1965 the first regular American ground troops were sent to South Vietnam, where American political, economic, and, increasingly, military interests had been trying to prop up an anti-Communist regime since the 1950s. By 1968 there were a half million U.S. troops in South Vietnam, a great many of them draftees. Although the draft has always been controversial in America, it was probably most troublesome during the Vietnam years. Indeed, it is quite likely that the controversies over the Vietnam-era draft inspired Congress to allow the Cold War draft, in effect since 1948, to expire in 1973.

Young Americans resisted the Vietnam-era draft for many reasons. Some found the war itself illegal, since war had never been declared by Congress as the Constitution stipulates. Others simply found the war unjust or even pointless, claiming that America was interfering unduly in the affairs of a faraway Southeast Asian nation. Still others thought the draft itself unfair. Until 1971 all college students could get deferments. In general only those who were reasonably well off could go to college; the draft, as in the Civil War, fell mostly on poor whites, African Americans, and Latinos. Antiwar protests began in earnest in 1965, and over the next few years these protests often had an antidraft component. Many young men, for example, burned their draft cards as a form of protest. Others went underground if their number was called, or even sought asylum overseas. Tens of thousands, meanwhile, sought to attain conscientious objector status and, failing that, some went to prison rather than serve.

In 1970 the draft system was shifted to a lottery and, in 1971, the college deferments as well as most other exemptions were lifted. By then, however, fewer people were being drafted as the U.S. military commitment to Vietnam was being reduced. Some military leaders, for their part, were also wondering whether the draft provided the best possible military. By the early 1970s units made up of draftees were suffering severe problems of indiscipline, disdain for authority, and even drug use. Again, the draft bill was not renewed in 1973, ending the draft and beginning the shift to an all-volunteer military in the United States. To heal old wounds, President Gerald Ford gave amnesty in 1974 to most of those who had dodged the Vietnam-era draft. His successor, Jimmy Carter, renewed the requirement for young men ages eighteen to twenty-six to register with selective service, opening a new debate on the desirability or usefulness of a draft, but there has been no serious consideration on the part of the U.S. Congress to enact a new draft bill.

The End of the Cold War and a New Era

The Cold War wound down from 1989 to 1991, as the Communist regimes in Eastern Europe collapsed and as the Soviet Union itself disbanded and Russia began its shift toward democracy. With little need to maintain large standing armies or constant military readiness, most European countries ended conscription or drew it down, a process which continues. Only Germany, among the major European powers, maintains a large-scale draft. Elsewhere, the Middle Eastern nation of Israel perceives a constant need for military readiness, and it maintains one of the most extensive drafts of modern times. Young Israeli men are drafted for three years and even afterward are expected to remain in the reserves. Even Israeli women are drafted, in this case for two years. As always, however, Israel's draft is not without controversy. Many young Israelis express weariness with the perpetual militarization and tension of their lives while some servicepeople have become "refuseniks" because they will not serve in support of policies they find unfair or unjust.

In the United States, discussion of the draft could be heard again following the terrorist attacks of September 11, 2001, and as the country began its war in Iraq in 2003. Some envisioned a long-term commitment in Iraq and, possibly, elsewhere in the Middle East, and the draining fighting there has taken a heavy toll not only on the regular military but also on the National Guard and Reserves. Repeated tours of duty have become common, while loopholes in enlistment agreements have meant that, sometimes, even people who have been out of the service for years have been called back. Critics have referred to such measures as a backdoor draft, since they require some people to serve against their will. In 2003, and again in

2007, Congressman Charles Rangel tried to introduce a new draft bill, claiming that the current military is disproportionately made up of the poor and members of minority groups. Unlike during the Civil War or Vietnam era, however, this is the result of people joining the military in search of job training or college funding. Rangel also claims that a draft law which allowed no exemptions, in which the rich were called up as well as the poor, would encourage Americans to examine more seriously the military policies of their government. Otherwise it is too easy for people to remain distant and view such conflicts as the Iraq war abstractly.

Few leaders or commentators share Rangel's reasoning. His proposals have inspired reminders that the draft is a violation of personal liberty, is extremely expensive, and might not even provide the best, most useful, military force. Indeed, military leaders themselves quickly reject the possibility of a new draft, since it might well result in a large-scale force of relatively unskilled, marginally committed soldiers. The modern military requires high levels of technical skill and specialization that are much better supplied through trained volunteers, and recent calls for an increase in the military have been to provide funding for a larger volunteer force, not a drafted one. Although the U.S. government maintains the selective service bureaucracy, most believe that no new draft is likely anytime soon.

CHAPTER 1

The Military Draft from the French Revolution Through World War II

Chapter Preface

In earlier centuries, leaders built armies in various ways. These included the hiring of mercenaries; the use of forced, or "impressed" troops; and the levying of civilian militias. Beginning with the French Revolution in 1789, governments began to consider building armies through regular conscription. French spokesmen proclaimed that, now, all French people were full citizens, possessing all the rights and obligations that citizenship entailed. If the ability to vote and protection under the law were among those rights, then perhaps service in the military might be one of the obligations. For the French, a series of foreign wars from 1791 to 1815 also created a pressing need for a large military, and conscription was one of the ways to ensure that leaders had enough manpower to fulfill that need.

Following the French Revolution, many nations considered conscription using the same reasoning that the French had: the obligations of citizenship and military needs. Members of the U.S. Congress considered a draft during the War of 1812, although it was ultimately rejected on the grounds that a draft was a violation of the principle of individual liberty. In later decades, it was only during major wars that the United States had a draft. Each time, however, the draft was controversial. The Civil War draft of the 1860s inspired protests because it tended to draw in only the poor; those drafted could pay three hundred dollars to get an exemption or could find a substitute. When the United States entered World War I in 1917, millions were required to register for the draft as many leaders believed that a large army would not only satisfy military needs but encourage patriotism. Large-scale resistance, however, helped end the World War I draft by the end of 1918.

The first peacetime draft ever instituted in the United States came in 1940. That year, World War II was already underway in Europe and the Japanese threatened territorial advancement in Asia. Still, the 1940 draft bill only passed narrowly. Its supporters included those who claimed that the draft helped instill patriotism. Opponents included those who felt that a draft was a violation of civil liberties as well as those who rejected the use of violence to solve problems. Once the draft was underway, some of these opponents ended up in prison. Meanwhile, opposition to the draft was largely stilled as the United States entered World War II in December 1941. Some ten million men altogether were drafted, and they remained in uniform for the duration of the war rather than for a fixed period of time.

The First Modern Draft Was a National Call to Arms

Alan Forrest

Until just over two hundred years ago, armies in the western world were either professional, paid armies of various sorts, or they were voluntary or enforced (or "pressed") militias made up of ordinary citizens for a specific purpose. The first modern draft was a product of the French Revolutionary era which lasted in its entirety from 1789 to 1815. During those years French people seized the reigns of government for themselves, and they proclaimed that governments should reflect the will of the people. All people, now, were citizens with a direct interest in and obligations toward the welfare of the state and should share in the common defense in times of war. In the early 1790s, when France faced threats of invasion from European monarchies fearful of the spread of such democracy, the need for a citizen's army grew. The result was a levée *en masse, or mass conscription.*

In the following selection, historian Alan Forrest examines this first modern draft. He notes that it was designed to not only increase the size of the army but also to strengthen people's faith in the state that the revolutionaries were trying to build. Forrest is a professor of history at the University of York in the United Kingdom.

When the French decreed the *levée en masse* [mass conscription] on 23 August 1793, they were well aware that they were breaking with centuries of tradition and creating a new form of legitimation for the military demands of the state. The *levée* was based on the simple principle that the nation was the sovereign authority in the French Republic, and that the nation had the right to demand the performance of military service as one of the fundamental duties implicit in the enjoyment of citizenship. No precedent that posited citizenship as the basis for recruitment in this way could be cited—neither in the American Revolution nor in Cromwell's England nor in the Roman republic so lauded in the writings of the Enlightenment and in the speeches of [French Revolutionary leader] Maximilien Robespierre.

The revolutionaries were here venturing into the unknown, breaking new ground in pursuit of liberty and idealism. Their revolution freed people from the constraints imposed on them during the *ancien régime*, [old, royal regime] doing so by a process of civic and political empowerment. In 1790 a patriotic society composed of shopkeepers and artisans had been founded in Bordeaux to educate the mass of the population in their new rights and duties, arguing that "since every man is a member of the state, the new order of things can call anyone to the public administration." This was a heady notion in a society where public offices had been widely brought and sold, and where great swathes of government service had been the preserve of privilege and venality. The *levée en masse* would take the principle of universality further and apply it to the defense of the state. It must be seen as an experimental device operated against the background of *la patrie en danger*, [the nation threatened] of threatened invasion and national emergency, and in the face of much popular bitterness and suspicion about the soldier and his lot.

No Incentive to Serve

The revolutionaries were acknowledging that they could no longer rely on traditional mechanisms to produce an army of the size and quality that were needed, mechanisms that had served successive kings well, at least until the time of [King] Louis XV [1710–1774]. Old Regime armies had seldom lacked men, though the social status of soldiering was low, and the incentive to become an infantryman in the royal service was poor. Those who made a career in the armies knew that there were few opportunities for promotion, officers' batons being reserved for those with aristocratic credentials, and that when their careers were over, often cut short by wounds and fevers, there would be no pension to offer them some security in their declining years. The image of the old soldier who returned to his village broken by war, with no family or small-holding, reduced to begging and petty crime, was a familiar one in the eighteenth-century French countryside. It helps explain the many demands made in the *cahiers de doléances* [prerevolutionary list of grievances] for an immediate improvement in the conditions of military service—an end to social privilege in the army, a guarantee that soldiers receive their pay on time, a desire that French troops should not be forced to beg and plunder to keep themselves alive.

Many had no alternative but to serve. Indeed, [historian] André Corvisier calculated that, at the peak of [King] Louis XIV's [1638–1715] wars, around one Frenchman in six was called on to bear arms at some time during his life, though not necessarily to participate in actual warfare. An outbreak of banditry or the appearance of wolves in a rural area could equally result in a call to arms. But few rushed to offer their services. The armies relied heavily on the poor, among them beggars and vagabonds consigned to the public infirmaries and poor houses by a state increasingly concerned with the needs of internal order. Such men were often prepared to enlist in return for the recruitment bounty and the promise of a livelihood. Others were recruited by methods reminiscent of the press-gang, as recruiting officers toured provincial fairs and markets, first banging drums and hoisting flags at local *fêtes* [festivals] and then seizing drunken revellers before they sobered up sufficiently to realize what was happening to them. The armies also depended on foreign mercenaries to a degree that the nationalist ideology of the Revolution could not accept. For Louis XIV, mercenaries had been a welcome additional source of manpower that presented him with neither practical nor moral dilemmas; indeed, between the Dutch Wars [1672–1678] and the Peace of Ryswick [1697] there had never been fewer than 25 percent of mercenary troops in the French infantry, and 22 percent in the army as a whole. Even in 1789 there were still twenty-three foreign regiments serving Louis XVI [1754–1793] recruited from among the traditional mercenaries of the European continent, the Swiss, the Germans, and the Irish.

Militia Service

In times of grave peril, the government supplemented military numbers by levying militia service on the population at large—a highly unpopular practice that routinely dragged young men away from their farms and workshops for six years at a time. The militia system was seen as unfair and divisive, a kind of lottery in which an individual's future and self-respect were callously gambled away, and one, moreover, from which the rich and privileged, along with their servants and lackeys, were usually exempt. Such institutions cried out for reform, as [French official] Joseph Servan noted in a memorable pamphlet published in 1780, prophetically entitled *Le Soldat-citoyen [The Citizen-Soldier]*, in which he offered solutions to the abuses he saw all around him. In Servan's view, it was simply too easy to claim, as many did in the eighteenth century, that the quality of French troops must always be high because of the inherent excellence of French national character, education, and government. Nor was it realistic to assert that the country's history and traditions had always served it well in military matters. In reality, Servan argued, France had seen a real militia, based upon principles of communal self-defense, give way first to a feudal levy, and finally to a system of paid vigilantism, "the least good of the three." While the resulting system might have passed for a deeply ingrained part of French military culture under the *ancien régime*, it was incontestably unwieldy and inefficient militarily. After 1789, it would prove incompatible with the needs of a revolutionary nation that believed itself to be under threat of extinction. . . .

The *levée en masse* was not the first innovatory recruitment measure taken by the revolutionaries, though it was the first distinctively Jacobin [a left-wing revolutionary group] one. The draining away of men from the line regiments and the prestige that attached to the new, more patriotic National Guard units had begun to alter the image of soldiering as early as 1789, even though the mutinies at [the town of] Nancy and elsewhere during 1790 had cast doubt on the old system of discipline in a world where soldiers, too, could claim civic rights and even privileges. In garrison towns along the northern frontier, for instance, troops were already denouncing unpopular officers and forging links with patriots and popular societies in the local population, and in Cherbourg the club demanded the dismissal of the entire general staff and the replacement of all nobles who still held military commands.

The Draft Arrives

Faced with the rapid extension of the war in March 1793, the government could not but seek new methods of recruitment to boost numbers and morale. The call for volunteers and the creation of new volunteer regiments—the preferred solution in 1791 and 1792—was no longer seen as adequate to the scale of the crisis; and while a major call-up in the spring of 1793 (known as the *levée des 300,000*) eventually produced the numbers required, it also gave rise to bitter resentments. For the first time, the government introduced quotas to reflect local population figures, demanding that each department, each district, eventually each town or village should produce an appropriate number of men for the army. But the method of choosing them was not laid down by law. Some communities used a form of balloting, which at least seemed fair. Regardless of method, however, the choice often fell on men regarded as marginal to village life—shepherds working on isolated hillsides, the indigent from the local poorhouses, and even migrant workers who had the misfortune to pass through when the levy was being raised. There were too many exemptions, too many privileged jobs in the civil administration, and too many opportunities for the rich to buy themselves out of serving in person. Desertion and draft-evasion followed, often with the open connivance of parents, mayors, and entire communities. The Jacobin's demand that all must be equally liable for service had a practical, as well as an ideological, justification.

That the policy was largely successful can be seen in the results achieved by French arms in the months that followed, when the war along the northern and eastern frontiers was effectively turned around, and foreign forces were pushed back from French soil. It was reflected also in the size of the force assembled, which, if it never reached the figure of three quarters of a million that was intended, produced an army of over 600,000 men, far larger than the forces disposed of by France's enemies at that time. This enormous army was at the heart of all France's military successes for the rest of the decade and was not properly replenished until full-blown annual conscription was introduced under the Jourdan Law of September 1798. There were, it is true, some small, partial levies in the intervening years, especially for the cavalry, but they were half-hearted affairs, announced as exceptional and deeply resented by large parts of the population. Essentially it would be the army of the Year II, [September 1793 to September 1794 of the French revolutionary calendar], weakened by casualties, sickness, and desertion, that would go on to fight the military campaigns of the Directory, conquer Italy, set up "sister republics" in Holland and Switzerland, and carry [Napoleon] Bonaparte to the banks of the Nile. Its successes in battle, and the wholly unprecedented glamour that accrued to the army as a result, go far to explain the mystique that the ideal of a citizen-army came to command, not just in France but among the Revolution's many enemies as well.

Citizenship Requires Service

Nevertheless, the myth of the *levée en masse* cannot be explained in military terms alone. The success of the recruitment campaign and the victories registered by the armies it produced might inspire respect and admiration, mingled with some astonishment from those who had warned that such drastic restructuring could not work in an institution that was critically dependent on discipline and obedience. Other armies had dazzled before in the history of European warfare, without leaving such a deeply engrained cultural legacy. It was the boldness of the patriotic vision of August 1793, not just the tactical proficiency of the army it engendered, that explains the power of the myth and its durability. The clarion call was nationalism and the obligation of every citizen to render service to the nation, a principle welcomed for its own sake by revolutionary militants, especially the leadership of the Paris sections and the Jacobin Club, where it immediately acquired far-reaching ideological significance. The *levée en masse*, in contrast to the partial levies that preceded it, did not base itself upon traditional categories of social distinction. All, in theory at least, had a duty to perform, one that they owed to their country and their fellow-citizens rather than to the person of the king or to any local *seigneu* [noble]. The *patrie* had been declared *en danger*, and the whole people of France were mobilized for their own defense. While age, gender, or marital status might excuse most Frenchmen from front-line service, all had a role to play. This is captured in the resonance of the first words of the decree, which spelled out that:

> henceforth, until the enemies have been driven from the territory of the Republic, the French people are in permanent

requisition for army service. The young men shall go to battle; the married men shall forge arms and transport provisions; the women shall make tents and clothes, and shall serve in the hospitals; the children shall turn old linen into lint; the old men shall repair to the public places, to stimulate the courage of the warriors and preach the unity of the Republic and the hatred of kings.

The Republic itself was compared to a city under siege, and the territory of France to a huge military camp, where national property and the abandoned houses of those who had emigrated should be turned into barracks, with public squares reconstituted as public workshops, all in the cause of the war and victory.

In short, war was to be a total effort, in which all members of the community had a role. All were to be mobilized in the common good until such time as France's enemies had been driven off and defeated. This effort was consistent with the principle laid down in the Jacobin constitution of 24 June 1793, which declared that all were equally at the service of the state: [and that] "all Frenchmen are soldiers: all have training in handling arms." The fact that the rich could no longer buy themselves out of serving in person was a powerful element in the *levée*'s appeal. Personal circumstance, not status or income level, determined who should march first. "Unmarried citizens or childless widowers from eighteen to twenty-five years shall go first," proclaimed the law. Public officials were allowed to remain at their posts, a provision that occasioned some bitterness among those called to the colors. But otherwise all were equal before the recruiting-sergeant, even if all were not wanted for active service. This was what the ordinary people of France understood by "the nation in arms," the slogan emblazoned on a banner carried by each new battalion, which proclaimed it the representative of "the French people risen against tyrants."

A Government of Free People Cannot Enact a Draft

Daniel Webster

In 1814 when the prominent American statesman Daniel Webster made the speech excerpted in this selection, the United States was still a very young nation. It had just ended the inconclusive War of 1812 against Great Britain. Among the important issues of that war were the forced "impressments," or draft, of hundreds of American sailors into the British navy and the continued British possession of Canada. Much of the fighting on the American side, as in the Revolutionary War (1775–1883), was done by voluntary citizen's militias. However, some of the individual states, notably those of New England, refused to provide either militias or funding to the national war effort. It was in this context that the national government made its first attempt to institute a draft.

Webster, as the selection indicates, strongly opposed the attempt. He argued that the U.S. Constitution gives the government the right to raise armies, but not by means of a mandatory draft. To him, such measures were a violation of the principles of liberty on which the United States was founded. Webster served for many decades as both congressman and senator in the first half of the nineteenth century. He also served twice as secretary of state, and he ran unsuccessfully for president three times.

L et us examine the nature & extent of the power, which is assumed by the various military measures before us. In the present want of men & money, the Secretary of War [now secretary of defense] has proposed to Congress a Military Conscription. For the conquest of Canada, the people will not en-

Daniel Webster, "An Unpublished Speech on the Conscription Bill, U.S. House of Representatives, December 9, 1814," from *The Letters of Daniel Webster*, edited by C.H. Van Tyne, New York: McClure, Phillips, and Co., 1902.

list; & if they would, the Treasury is exhausted, & they could not be paid. Conscription is chosen as the most promising instrument, both of overcoming reluctance to the Service, & of subduing the difficulties which arise from the deficiencies of the Exehequer [part of government responsible for collecting revenue]. The administration asserts the right to fill the ranks of the regular army by compulsion. It contends that it may now take one out of every twenty-five men, & any part or the whole of the rest, whenever its occasions require. Persons thus taken by force, & put into an army, may be compelled to serve there, during the war, or for life. They may be put on any service, at home or abroad, for defence or for invasion, according to the will & pleasure of Government. This power does not grow out of any invasion of the country, or even out of a state of war. It belongs to Government at all times, in peace as well as in war, & is to be exercised under all circumstances, according to its mere discretion. This, Sir, is the amount of the principle contended for by the Secretary of War.

Is this, Sir, consistent with the character of a free Government? Is this civil liberty? Is this the real character of our Constitution? No, Sir, indeed it is not. The Constitution is libelled, foully libelled. The people of this country have not established for themselves such a fabric of despotism. They have not purchased at a vast expense of their own treasure & their own blood a Magna Carta [great charter or agreement] to be slaves. Where is it written the Constitution, in what article or section is it contained, that you may take children from their parents, & parents from their children, & compel them to fight the battles of any war, in which the folly or the wickedness of Government may engage it? Under what concealment has this power lain hidden, which now for the first time comes forth, with a tremendous & baleful aspect, to trample down & destroy the dearest rights of personal liberty? Who will show me any constitutional injunction, which makes it the duty of the American people to surrender every thing valuable in life,

& even life itself, not when the safety of their country & its liberties may demand the sacrifice, but whenever the purposes of an ambitious & mischievous Government may require it? Sir, I almost disdain to go to quotations & references to prove that such an abominable doctrine has no foundation in the Constitution of the country. It is enough to know that that instrument was intended as the basis of a free Government, & that the power contended for is incompatible with any notion of personal liberty. An attempt to maintain this doctrine upon the provisions of the Constitution is an exercise of perverse ingenuity to extract slavery from the substance of a free Government. It is an attempt to show, by proof & argument, that we ourselves are subjects of despotism, & that we have a right to chains & bondage, firmly secured to us & our children, by the provisions of our Government. It has been the labor of other men, at other times, to mitigate & reform the powers of Government by construction; to support the rights of personal security by every species of favorable & benign interpretation, & thus to infuse a free spirit into Governments, not friendly in their general structure & formation to public liberty.

A Draft Is Slavery

The supporters of the measures before us act on the opposite principle. It is their task to raise arbitrary powers, by construction, out of a plain written charter of National Liberty. It is their pleasing duty to free us of the delusion, which we have fondly cherished, that we are the subjects of a mild, free & limited Government, & to demonstrate by a regular chain of premises & conclusions, that Government possesses over us a power more tyrannical, more arbitrary, more dangerous, more allied to blood & murder, more full of every form of mischief, more productive of every sort & degree of misery, than has been exercised by any civilized Government, with a single exception, in modern times.

The Secretary of War has favored us with an argument on the constitutionality of this power. Those who lament that such doctrines should be supported by the opinion of a high officer of Government, may a little abate their regret, when they remember that the same officer, in his last letter of instructions to our ministers abroad, maintained the contrary. In that letter, he declares, that even the impressment of seamen, for which many more plausible reasons may be given than for the impressment of soldiers, is repugnant to our constitution.

It might therefore be a sufficient answer to his argument, in the present case, to quote against it the sentiments of its own author, & to place the two opinions before the House [of Representatives] in a state of irreconcilable conflict. Further comment on either might then be properly forborne, until he should be pleased to inform us which he retracted, & to which he adhered. But the importance of the subject may justify a further consideration of the argument.

Congress having, by the Constitution a power to raise armies, the Secretary contends that no restraint is to be imposed on the exercise of this power, except such as is expressly stated in the written letter of the instrument. In other words, that Congress may execute its powers, by any means it chooses, unless such means are particularly prohibited. But the general nature & object of the Constitution impose as rigid a restriction on the means of exercising power, as could be done by the most explicit injunctions. It is the first principle applicable to such a case that no construction shall be admitted which impairs the general nature & character of the instrument. A free constitution of Government is to be construed upon free principles, & every branch of its provisions is to receive such an interpretation as is full of its general spirit. No means are to be taken by implication, which would strike us absurdly, if expressed. And what would have been more absurd, than for this constitution to have said, that to secure the great blessings of liberty it gave to Government an uncontrolled power of military conscription? Yet such is the absurdity which it is made to exhibit, under the commentary of the Secretary of War.

Government's Power Are Limited

But it is said, that it might happen that an army would not be raised by voluntary enlistment, in which case the power to raise armies would be granted in vain, unless they might be raised by compulsion. If this reasoning could prove any thing, it would equally show, that whenever the legitimate powers of the Constitution should be so badly administered as to cease to answer the great ends intended by them, such new powers may be assumed or usurped, as any existing administration may deem expedient. This is a result of his own reasoning, to which the Secretary does not profess to go. But it is a true result. For if it is to be assumed, that all powers were granted, which might by possibility become necessary, & that Government itself is the judge of this possible necessity, then the powers of Government are precisely what it chooses they should be. Apply the same reasoning to any other power granted to Congress, & test its accuracy by the result. Congress has power to borrow money. How is it to exercise this power? Is it confined to voluntary loans? There is no express limitation to that effect, &, in the language of the Secretary, it might happen, indeed, it has happened, that persons could not be found willing to lend. Money might be borrowed then in any other mode. In other words, Congress might resort to a *forced* loan. It might take the money of any man, by force, & give him in exchange Exchequer notes or Certificate of Stock. Would this be quite constitutional, Sir? It is entirely within the reasoning of the Secretary, & it is a result of his argument, outraging the rights of individuals in a far less degree, than the practical consequences which he himself draws from it. A compulsory loan is not to be compared, in point of enormity, with a compulsory military service.

If the Secretary of War has proved the right of Congress to enact a law enforcing a draft of men out of the Militia into the regular army, he will at any time be able to prove, quite as clearly, that Congress has power to create a Dictator. The arguments which have helped him in one case, will equally aid him in the other. The same reason of a supposed or possible state necessity, which is urged now, may be repeated then, with equal pertinency & effect.

Sir, in granting Congress the power to raise armies, the People have granted all the means which are ordinary & usual, & which are consistent with the liberties & security of the People themselves; & they have granted no others. To talk about the unlimited power of the Government over the means to execute its authority, is to hold a language which is true only in regard to despotism. The tyranny of Arbitrary Government consists as much in its means as in its ends; & it would be a ridiculous & absurd constitution which should be less cautious to guard against abuses in the one case than in the other. All the means & instruments which a free Government exercises, as well as the ends & objects which it pursues, are to partake of its own essential character, & to be conformed to its genuine spirit. A free Government with arbitrary means to administer it is a contradiction; a free Government without adequate provision for personal security is an absurdity; a free Government, with an uncontrolled power of military conscription, is a solecism [fundamental mistake] at once the most ridiculous & abominable that ever entered into the head of man.

Antidraft Riots Bring Chaos to Civil War–era New York City

Barnet Schechter

During the American Civil War, fought from 1861 to 1865, both sides instituted a mandatory draft, the first in America's history. The Confederacy of the southern states enacted a draft law in April 1862. Facing a manpower shortage, the northern and most western states, the so-called Union, passed its own draft law in March 1863. It subjected men ages eighteen to thirty-five to possible conscription. However, a payment of three hundred dollars, a quite substantial amount in those days, could secure exemption from the draft. This exemption convinced many that only the poor were subject to the draft and that the rich could simply buy their way out.

In the following selection, historian Barnet Schechter describes the New York City riots begun by those who objected to the idea of a "rich man's war being fought by poor men" as some put it. Many of the rioters were recent immigrants from Ireland who objected not only to compulsory service but also to the notion that they were fighting for the freedom of slaves. Many feared that freed African American slaves would compete with them in the labor market. Schechter is the author of two other books, The Battle for New York *and* The City at the Heart of the American Revolution.

With an orderly crowd filling the draft office, Provost Marshal Charles Jenkins had set the lottery wheel in motion at the Forty-sixth Street draft office at 10 a.m., and in the next half hour a blindfolded clerk pulled about seventy-five names, which Jenkins read aloud. He recalled, "Everything went on quietly, and I began to hope that no attack would be made." Then Peter Masterson's Black Joke Engine Company arrived with its steam engine and the men dressed in their firefighting gear. A pistol shot rang out like a starting gun, a hail of paving stones crashed through the draft office windows, and the firemen, supported by the crowd, surged forward.

Shouting "Down with the rich men!" the crowd stormed the draft office, setting it on fire and severely injuring several enrolling officers with clubs. "I stepped forward," Jenkins reported, "but was borne back by the mass, and pushed through the back door into the back yard, and took refuge in the next building." Without resorting to their guns, the Metropolitans [Metropolitan Police] fought off the rioters, enabling a federal marshal to lock the enrollment records in an iron safe that the rioters were unable to open or remove from the burning building.

While the bruised and battered policemen escaped from the burning draft office, and the fire spread to other buildings on that block, the mob outside hurled rocks and paving stones at [Colonel Robert] Nugent's fifty convalescent soldiers from the Invalid Corps who had belatedly converged on the scene. A round of blank cartridges did nothing to frighten the mob, so some of the soldiers, panicked and without orders, fired musket balls, which killed or wounded several rioters. Without time to reload, the soldiers were quickly disarmed by the enraged mob, which clubbed two of them to death with their own guns and chased a third to a rocky ledge near the East River and threw him off before dropping boulders on his lifeless body. These first casualties of the draft riots had barely survived the carnage of Civil War battlefields, only to meet their deaths on the Union home front.

Most of the Invalid Corps troops, however, escaped with varying degrees of injury. John Alcock was chased along Fortieth Street toward Second Avenue, where the mob "took his musket from his hands, and struck him with their fists, with stones, and with sticks, knocking him down, fracturing his skull, and breaking his left arm, and bruising his left side." Prone on the sidewalk, Alcock was kicked by Daniel Conroy, a forty-six-year-old laborer, and Thomas Kiernan, forty, a contractor, both Irish-born residents of the immediate area, who left him bleeding on the sidewalk.

Thomas Maguire, another Irish American, had Alcock carried into his store until the soldier could be evacuated to a hospital. When a few relentless rioters entered and clubbed Alcock on the head, Maguire hid him in the basement, covered in hay, and brought in a doctor to dress his wounds, which had "bled profusely." The police later rescued Alcock with a carriage.

New York's Poor Irish Immigrants

Soon a second phase of the riots began to unfold, as political protest combined with sabotage of government targets gave way to street crime and looting; attacks on individuals and private property were suddenly tempting in the chaotic atmosphere. On Lexington Avenue just below Forty-fifth Street, the rioters had set their sights on several three-story houses and were throwing cobblestones through the front windows while women and children fled out the back doors.

At 11:30 the six draft offices around the city received orders from Nugent to suspend work and transfer their records to Governors Island to keep them out of the clutches of the mob. Nugent also emptied his headquarters of all papers, weapons, and equipment, he wrote, "as the mob had threatened not only to hang me but destroy the building also."

Most of the mob surged down Third Avenue, preventing the various reinforcements sent by [Police superintendent] Kennedy from ever reaching the draft office at Forty-sixth Street. The Metropolitans coming up from the Broadway draft office clashed with the mob at Forty-fourth Street but were outnumbered and forced to retreat. Two more police detachments were similarly beaten in rapid succession and fell back, dragging their fallen comrades with them.

Sergeant Robert McCredie, known as "Fighting Mac," arrived with a fourth squad and was soon joined by a fifth. With fewer than fifty men—those from all five squads who had not yet been wounded—McCredie turned the tide and drove the rioters up to Forty-fifth Street. However, they turned our to be just the vanguard of the mob, and its full weight suddenly pressed forward down Third Avenue while more rioters poured in from the side streets, engulfing the police and scattering them southward again.

All of them were injured; McCredie was chased up the stoop of a building and, in the process of being beaten, rammed through the wooden panels of the front door. He managed to reach the second floor, where a German woman concealed him under a mattress and told his pursuers that he had fled through the window. When the mob torched the building, the woman carried McCredie on her back all the way to Lexington Avenue, where a cab took him to a police station. She had saved his life, but the mob had disabled one of the department's most effective officers.

While the police were battling the rioters on Third Avenue, clusters of men, women, and children from the city's slums filtered northward and looted hungrily, with few policemen to stop them. Set in motion by the draft and Democratic denunciations of excessive federal and state power, the metaphor of class warfare—exploited for decades by Democrats like Fernando Wood and Isaiah Rynders to garner immigrant votes—had become a literal, violent eruption, far bigger than any they had provoked before. . . .

The Poor Against the Rich

Around the city, scenes unfolded that revealed the chasm between New York's social classes—and how deeply the antidraft rioters craved equal treatment at a time when the poor lacked the most basic amenities. "Turn out; turn out by six o'clock, or we'll burn you in your beds!" a rioter shouted from the basement of St. Luke's Hospital at Fifth Avenue and Fifty-fifth Street, threatening some one hundred sick and wounded soldiers. The "huge, hatless laborer, with his sleeves rolled up to the armpits, bare-breasted, red with liquor and rage, strode up and down the hall," according to Eliza Woolsey Howland, who served beside her sisters as a nurse caring for Union troops.

"But a wounded rioter (shot, with a brick-bat in his hand), was about this time brought by a crowd to the hospital door, promptly admitted, and kindly cared for" by the Reverend Dr. William Muhlenberg, the founder and director of the charitable hospital. An "elderly man . . . with a noble face, white hair and wonderful dark eyes," Muhlenberg then left the rioter's bedside and went outside to speak with the mob. Explaining that his hospital was open to anyone who needed treatment, he asked if they would still "threaten this house with fire and storm."

The crowd responded with shouts of "No, no; long live St. Luke's," and established a "vigilance committee" to defend the hospital. "As he braved alone that howling mob of men and women, and by his personal magnetism quieted their rage," Howland wrote, "it was like the picture of the working of a miracle by a mediaeval saint."

"It was now noon, but the hot July sun was obscured by heavy clouds, that hung in ominous shadows over the city," [journalist Joel Tyler] Headley wrote, "while from near Cooper Institute to Forty-Sixth Street, or about thirty blocks, [Third Avenue] was black with human beings—house-tops, windows, and stoops all filled with rioters or spectators. Dividing it like a stream, horse-cars arrested in their course lay strung along as far as the eye could reach. As the glance ran along this mighty mass of men and women north, it rested at length on huge columns of smoke rolling heavenward from burning buildings." Of the estimated fifty thousand people on Third Avenue, most were spectators, but about ten thousand were actively rioting. Of the latter, several thousand prevented the fire department's chief engineer, John Decker, and his men from getting near the draft office with their equipment, despite the fact that poor, mostly German families lived in the upper stories and adjacent buildings.

While these women and children fled the blaze and lost their belongings, John Andrews, the Copperhead [members of the governing Democratic Party who opposed the war] lawyer from Virginia briefly tailed by the police the night before, kept the crowd stirred up with a harangue against the draft. "'You must organize, boys.' (Cries of 'That's the talk,' 'You're the boy, my chicken,' &c.) 'You must organize and keep together, and appoint leaders, and crush this damned abolition draft into the dust.' (Tremendous cheering.) . . . 'If you don't find any one to lead you, by Heaven! I will do it myself.' (Great sensation and applause.)" Many in the crowd wondered who the speaker was, and when someone said it was [newspaperman] Ben Wood, Andrews was cheered even more enthusiastically.

At about 12:30, when chief engineer Decker managed to address the rioters, he expressed sympathy with their objections to the draft but pleaded with them to step aside and let him save the property of residents who had nothing to do with it. Hoping to contain the mayhem he had sparked, Black Joke foreman Peter Masterson supported Decker's appeal, and the cheering crowd parted momentarily, but a more aggressive mob returned to the scene and kept the firefighrers back. When the crowd shifted its attention to plundering stores and homes, the fire engines were put to use, but almost the entire block was consumed. . . .

The Rioting Spreads

The uptown mob had continued to grow as it surged southward on Third Avenue from Forty-sixth Street, picking up new members from smaller groups that had been dispersed by the police in other parts of the city. Clusters of people from the various slums "where the low Irish dwelt," according to Headley, continued to appear on almost every street corner, lured by news of looting. Having routed five squads of Metropolitans, the main mass of about ten thousand rioters had continued south to Thirty-fifth Street, where smaller groups pillaged the side streets while the mob paused and selected its next major target. "To the armory! To the armory," shouted the rioters.

It was widely known that Mayor [George] Opdyke and his son-in-law owned a warehouse on the northeast corner of Second Avenue and Twenty-first Street, a former piano factory, of which the top three floors contained the state armory. The local precinct commander had already sent some policemen to guard the five hundred guns and stores of ammunition. Just one block north stood the Union Steam Works, which had been converted to manufacture army carbines and contained more than four thousand of the short rifles. A small police guard had arrived there too.

When an attack on the state armory appeared imminent, thirty-two men from the elite "Broadway Squad" were assigned there and equipped with carbines as well as their pistols and locust clubs. The squad was based in the Central Office precinct, and its men were picked for their height and strength. Aware of the policemen inside, the crowd of several thousand rioters hesitated at the doors of the armory. Then, just after 1 p.m., having failed to set fire to the large brick building, the rioters pelted the windows and doors with rocks and gunfire. When several rioters charged and began breaking down the doors, the policemen shot them dead with their revolvers. As the standoff continued, the sergeant in charge succeeded in calling for reinforcements, but the precinct commander had none to send.

America's World War I Draft Was a Response to a Changed World

John Whiteclay Chambers II

World War I, fought from 1914 to 1918, was the first major modern conflict to be fought by armies which had been mostly drafted. It began in Europe but spread quickly; although the United States hoped at first to remain out of the conflict, attacks by German submarines on American ships brought the United States into the war in 1917 on the side of Great Britain, France, and their allies. Three and a half million American troops fought in the conflict and, as John Whiteclay Chambers II, the author of the following selection notes, nearly three-quarters of them were drafted.

America's only other experience with a draft, during the Civil War, had been violent and insecure. Chambers examines how, sixty years later, the world had changed in ways which made a draft both desirable and necessary to many American leaders. At the heart of the movement to begin a draft was the so-called preparedness movement, which argued that the United States had to be ready to accept a new role in this world. This new role required a larger military. Chambers is professor of history at Rutgers University.

America's painful Civil War experience with limited national conscription made it all the more surprising that in World War I, the federal government chose from the beginning to rely upon a national draft to raise the wartime army. The conscripted doughboys [soldiers] who filled the *Leviathan*

John Whiteclay Chambers II, from *To Raise an Army: The Draft Comes to Modern America*, New York: The Free Press, 1987.

when it steamed out of New York Harbor in the spring of 1918 were the first of millions of draftees to serve overseas. In the Civil War, fewer than 8 percent of the Union Army were draftees. In World War I, 72 percent of the 3.5 million citizen-soldiers were conscripted. Instead of relying upon individual choice and the operation of the market system as earlier, in 1917 the United States established a comprehensive draft and the Selective Service System. In 1918 this agency prohibited voluntary enlistment as inefficient and disruptive. Little wonder that contemporaries described the change in American military policy as "revolutionary."

Some supporters portrayed the World War I draft as inevitable—a consequence of the modernization of American institutions. In the midst of congressional debate over the draft act in April 1917, Henry Watterson, renowned editor of the *Louisville* (Ky.) *Courier-Journal*, declared:

> The volunteer system, like the stagecoach, served its purpose in primitive times, but like that stagecoach, it proved unequal to the expanding needs of modern time. . . . [The people] know that the volunteer system has been a failure wherever tried, and seeking efficiency they prefer the selective draft system, just as seeking speed they would prefer a locomotive to an oxcart.

It was an alluring metaphor. Watterson equated the draft with modernization, linking organizational change to technological development and describing both as indicators of progress. Yet such a description ignored the continued importance of the local volunteer tradition, even at the price of complete national military efficiency. As the editor of a rival Louisville paper, the *Evening Post*, responded: "The volunteer system [is] the very life of American democracy. The conscript system means the subjugation of America to military oligarchy such as that which has cursed Germany." Since the draft was adopted and successfully implemented without subjugating America to any such military oligarchy, many have accepted the position of contemporaries like Watterson who portrayed it as an inevitable and desirable development for the effective use of force in defense of American ideals and interests against aggressive major powers like Germany, a necessary aspect of a great nation's "modernization" in the early 20th century.

But who were the agents of this "modernization"? What were their motives? What were the results of the adoption of the draft? To the extent that historians have identified those responsible for the 1917 draft, they have differed over whether primary responsibility belongs to President Woodrow Wilson, ex-President Theodore Roosevelt, Maj. Gen. Leonard Wood (the "prophet of preparedness"), Maj. Gen. Hugh L. Scott, army chief of staff from 1914 to 1917, or Maj. Gen. Enoch H. Crowder, the judge advocate general who wrote the draft law and became wartime head of the Selective Service System. Also controversial is the role of the "preparedness" movement of 1915–17.

The core goal of this elite-dominated, multi-faceted social movement for greater military "preparedness" was a national mass conscript reserve army raised and prepared through universal military training and service (UMT&S). Like the continental European nations, the United States would have a pre-trained mass army of citizen reservists, trained and commanded by regulars and coordinated by a general staff. Unlike the major European forces, however, training would be for six months rather than two years and thus there would be no mass standing army in peacetime. Although it lasted from 1915 to 1920, the campaign for UMT&S reached such intensity between 1916 and 1917 that it became a virtual conscription crusade.

A New American Military

The movement's leading spokespeople—ex-president Roosevelt and General Wood, army chief of staff from 1910 to 1914—and such leading preparedness organizations as the National

Security League and the Military Training Camps Association (named "Platts-burgers" after the site of their original training camp) advocated complete reorganization of the traditional military format. As champions of nationalism and a stronger central government, they rejected both the militia and the U.S. Volunteers as anachronistic remnants of a parochialism obstructive to national efficiency and progress, which, they believed, required a single, unitary, national military force.

Although the regular army represented such a force, it was not sufficient for these modernizers. With only 100,000 soldiers, it was too small to be effective against a first-class power. Even when supplemented by the 112,000 "ready reserves" of the National Guard, the ground forces of the United States were only slightly larger than those of Mexico or Belgium, and insignificant compared to the prewar forces of Germany or France. Before the outbreak of war in 1914, these two world powers had mass conscript standing armies of 800,000 which could be raised to 2 million within a few weeks by calling up units of young first-line reservists, and subsequently more than quadrupled by summoning millions of older men organized in second-line reserves.

American conscriptionists believed that reliance upon the regular army was not simply militarily inadequate but economically inefficient. Partly because it had to compete with civilian wage rates which were higher than in most other nations, the U.S. Army was the most expensive force, per soldier, in the world. Although American regulars were paid only $15 a month in 1914, the annual cost of maintaining each soldier was $1,700. This helps explain why, despite an annual expenditure of $200 million, which amounted to more than one-quarter of the federal budget, the United States had the smallest standing army among the great powers. The preparedness movement proposed a more cost-efficient instrument than the regular army as a means of increasing the size of the ground forces without a prohibitive increase in cost.

They proposed a severely modified version of the European mass-conscript-reservist army, in which the emphasis would be on shortterm training and national reserve organizations rather than on maintaining a large standing army. Each year 600,000 able-bodied, 18-year-old American males would spend six months in military training camps. The best of these would be selected for additional training as reserve officers. All would be assigned to geographically organized reserve units. During their civilian careers, the citizen-reservists would also progress, as they grew older, from first-line to second-line and, ultimately, into inactive reserves. Under the conscriptionists proposals, reservists could not be drafted into military service except in case of war or other national emergency.

From Reserves to Line Troops

The idea was to employ a small regular army for training and leadership and continued constabulary and garrison duty but to replace the old locally oriented and led National Guard and U.S. Volunteers with these new nationally oriented pretrained reserves. Universal military training and service (UMT&S) would be defined as a military obligation of citizenship. Consequently, the trainees would not be paid during training or their extended period in the reserves. Nor would there be enlistment bonuses in wartime, since the government would simply call up the millions of reservists. Citizen-soldiers, conscriptionists believed, should not expect compensation merely for fulfilling their duty to the nation. The result would be a large reserve force without a proportionate increase in the cost of the military establishment.

Scholars continue to disagree about the nature of the preparedness movement and its relationship to international and domestic developments. Differences also remain over the necessity and success of the draft of 1917. As the present study shows, the preparedness movement, like the new military doctrines and technology, were important in the evolution of this new military format, but the adoption of the *Nation-State Model: Wartime Mass Mobilization* was, more significantly, the result of larger changes in the structure of power relationships and attitudes within American society and the world.

If military institutions reflect the larger society, they should be affected by significant changes in that society. Certainly, the progressive era was a time of pivotal changes. By the turn of the century, mass production was creating new centers for labor and immense new sources of wealth. Dramatically expanding trade created an increasingly interdependent national and even international economy. Industrialization provided an opportunity in which new elites came to power in industry, transportation, and finance, and in the law firms, trade associations, and other institutions which assisted the giant new corporations. Seeing the new industrialism as the major source of personal and national wealth, these new corporate and professional elites sought to ensure a politico-economic environment conducive to the evolving system of big business and domestic and international interests.

Industrialization, Immigration, and Internationalism

Industrialization, of course, created major social problems. Millions of largely poor, agrarian workers immigrated from southern and eastern Europe, and the influx of so many Roman Catholics and Orthodox Jews triggered a renewed wave of nativism in America. Rapid industrialization also led to widespread poverty, crime, and disease in urban slums. While urbanization and industrialization greatly increased the wealth of the rich and expanded opportunities for many in the middle class, it also exacerbated the gap between the rich and the poor, and increased ethnic and regional tensions. Increasing social unrest and regional protest was aggravated by the depression of the 1890s and the consolidation of big business at the turn of the century.

As a result of these developments, many Americans began to modify their belief in unrestrained individualism, laissez-faire, and the self-regulating marketplace. They turned in varying degrees to collective action and often to the government for assistance in ameliorating social problems and enhancing their own economic position. This growing acceptance of active interventionism applied not simply to domestic circumstances but to international affairs as well. In the progressive era, the United States began to emerge as a world power, economically at least, projecting its influence into different areas of the world. In part this resulted from the growth of American industry and world trade, in part from an interventionism in which American presidents and foreign policy elites sought to go beyond simply reacting to external events, seeking instead to shape international affairs, particularly in the Caribbean and Central America, but also in East Asia, and Europe.

American interventionism was itself a reaction to major changes in the international system in the late 19th and early 20th centuries. A strong, unified yet politically unstable Germany challenged both the status quo and the balance of power. Imperialist European powers carved Africa into colonies and with expansionist Japan began to intervene in East Asia. Such imperialism threatened traditional U.S. interests in China and many Americans feared that the well-armed, aggressive imperialist powers, like Germany and Japan, might turn next to Latin America. To join the imperialist race or to defend American interests against it, internationally minded Americans sought to move beyond traditional political and military isolationism and pursue an active, interventionist foreign policy. Accordingly, American business people, diplomats, and presidents like Roosevelt, Taft, and Wilson began to play major roles in international diplomacy.

It was one segment of this new, internationally oriented, cosmopolitan expansionist elite which was responsible for the preparedness movement and its key military component, the conscription crusade. Departing from the American liberal tradition with its emphasis on commerce, rational behavior, and law as the tools of international relations, and the oceans and coastal defense as protection against external threats to national security, preparedness leaders saw an increasing need for extensive military and naval forces which could be projected overseas. An expanded military force was important, not merely for the emergency of the world war, but on a long-term continuing basis for the United States to defend its expanding interests and act as a major world power.

Selling America's World War II Draft

George Q. Flynn

Some sixteen million men served in the U.S. armed forces during World War II, as well as over 250,000 women. Of that total, ten million were drafted under the terms of the Burke-Wadsworth bill, which established America's first peacetime draft, as well as later modifications to it. These measures ultimately required all men between the ages of eighteen and thirty-eight to register with the Selective Service Administration and, if they were called up, to serve for the duration of the war. Altogether, around thirty-six million registered.

Such a massive mobilization would have been unthinkable in 1940, when the United States had not yet entered World War II and many people opposed a draft. In the following selection, historian George Q. Flynn describes some of the ways the military tried to ensure that public opinion supported a draft. Public relations efforts even stretched to the use of Hollywood films. Meanwhile, to show that the draft was truly democratic, even professional baseball players were subjected to it, although not without controversy. Flynn is a professor of history at Texas Tech University.

Draft officials went to extraordinary lengths during the first months of operation to insure that the system met the expectations of the American people. Chief among these expectations was that the draft represent a democratic approach to selection. With the draft a reality Col. John D. Langston reminded the War Department of the need "to mould public opinion in support of Selective Service." Above all he urged a constant stream of press releases on how well the system was doing.

As part of the selling campaign, the local communities and the War Department cooperated in staging elaborate ceremonies celebrating what the *New York Times* called "the pioneers of a mighty army." At Fort Dix, New Jersey, the first draftees were met at the train by a regimental band and a color guard. Down south Clyde O. Brown, a farm boy from Georgia, received the honor of representing the inductees from eight southern states. The governor and thousands of VIPs joined in the celebration. Unfortunately, Brown turned out to be no raw recruit but a grizzled veteran who had served several years in the infantry and been honorably discharged. Other promotional efforts included a comic strip entitled "Draftie." [Movie stars] Bob Hope and Dorothy Lamour appeared in a movie called *Caught in the Draft*, which one critic called a "wacky farce" on the futility of avoiding the call. A public poll in December 1940 showed that 92 percent of the population felt the draft was being handled fairly and 89 percent thought it was a good idea. A year earlier only 35 percent had approved of the idea. A poll of draft age males found 76 percent approving the draft. Older people felt it would help the boys mature and solve the unemployment problem.

Building on the good will, Selective Service publicized the effect of the draft on both the low and the mighty in American society. Americans laughed to read that young King Peter of Nazi-occupied Yugoslavia vowed never to dance again until his nation was free. But in New York City, Wong Yee Choy, a Chinese baker who spoke no English, was so anxious to fight the Nazis that he volunteered as the first draftee at local board number 1. Press coverage also followed the appearance of Benson Ford, Henry Ford's grandson, before a local board. His rejection for physical reasons was announced to the world, as was a deferment for Nelson Rockefeller. But Selective Service inducted William McChesney Martin, the president of the New York Stock Exchange. He exchanged his salary of $4,000 a month for a private's pay of $21 a month. The *New York*

Times editorialized that the public needed assurance that the draft was "absolutely democratic and made no distinction between men of different social ranks or economic status." Information used for claiming deferments became public knowledge.

The Wealthy and Famous Go Too

The press and public took a lively interest in the draft status of athletic heroes and movie stars. When the draft first began, baseball owners offered the usual expression of patriotic pieties. Warren Giles of Cincinnati swore that the star would "go just as quickly as the bat boy," and that baseball wanted no special treatment. Harry Grabiner of the White Sox, however, pointed out that the public still needed some amusement. Tom Yawkey of the Red Sox opposed exemptions but worried over the loss of Dom DiMaggio and Ted Williams. The owners voted on 11 December that any player subject to the draft should go on a national service list so that clubs interested in buying or selling such an individual would know of his vulnerability. Men on the list would not count against the club player limit.

Bob Feller of the Cleveland Indians and Phil Rizzuto of the Yankees were classified as 1-A [the draft top classification]. Probably no star received more attention than Hank Greenberg, the Detroit slugger and most valuable player. When first asked, Greenberg admitted being 1-A and insisted he would not ask for a deferment. Then reporters discovered that he had asked for an occupational deferment or a delay so he could play the entire season. The local board denied the application, and Greenberg, although 30 years old and scheduled to earn $55,000, was inducted. Fighter Joe Louis, the Brown Bomber, lost his dependent deferment when his wife began divorce proceedings. Joe reassured his fans that "I'm ready to go anytime. I'll take anything they give me." On a less serious note, in Austin, Minnesota, the star high school fullback had to leave town when his draft board reported he was playing under an assumed name and was in reality 23 years old.

As the stars began disappearing, several baseball owners began to reconsider their initial enthusiasm for the draft. Larry MacPhail of the Brooklyn Dodgers told the press that the draft was unfair to players, depriving them of a substantial income. In his opinion, baseball players should be given the same deferment privileges as scientists and physicians. Clark Griffith of the Washington Senators wrote to presidential aide Gen. Edwin M. Watson suggesting that a drill sergeant be assigned to each club so that the players could pick up military training while continuing to play. After all, he wrote, "baseball is a semi-public institution." At first Selective Service seemed receptive to such arguments and sent out a memo to local boards saying that players called for induction during the season might be granted a 60-day postponement because of hardship. But the public denounced such special treatment, and the War Department finally adopted a policy which allowed them to take some celebrities even if they failed to meet all standards, thus serving public opinion and preserving the myth of egalitarianism.

Support and Opposition

Preserving myths proved difficult because of the reality of the war. It was true that, of voters in their twenties, 86 percent favored the draft, while only 14 percent opposed it. But other polls showed that 90 percent of all youth were opposed to entering the war. A Youth Congress in Washington and a Youth Committee against War opposed the draft as a threat to civil liberties. Several divinity students in New York refused to register, and Norman Thomas, leader of the Socialist party, called for repeal of the law. In January 1941 5,000 students formed the Student Defenders of Democracy to resist induction.

Arguments against the draft ranged from threats to civil liberties to violations of the Constitution, although the Supreme Court had upheld the constitutionality of the draft in 1918. In 1941 the courts reaffirmed the right of the government to impose conscription even though there had been no declaration of war. The Third Circuit Court of Appeals held that the nation was "not precluded from preparing for battle ... until such time as our preparations would be too late." The court upheld the conviction of five draft objectors for failure to register. Legal protesters were few. More problems arose from those who simply tried to evade the system.

Selective Service relied more upon peer pressure than law to force men to cooperate, and sometimes the pressure bordered on vigilantism. In World War I civilians took suspects into custody for the police. Mass raids were conducted in some urban centers to round up men, who were then held until they could produce their draft cards. In November 1940 teams of volunteers assisted local boards in checking on men within the liable age categories. The director of the New York City draft used members of veteran organizations such as the American Legion to help. One official said "It will be a grand thing to get one conviction."

The Push to Create America's First Peacetime Draft Had Unforeseen Effects

J. Gary Clifford and Samuel R. Spencer Jr.

In the following selection, historians J. Gary Clifford and Samuel R. Spencer Jr. examine some of the legacies of America's first peacetime draft. The draft was the result of intense lobbying in 1940 by people who had ties to World War I's Plattsburg movement, which sought to create military training centers in the United States. These "Plattsburgers" helped to produce the Burke-Wadsworth Bill, passed in July 1940. It required all men between the ages of twenty-one and thirty-five to register for the draft. Any who were called up were selected by lottery.

In the summer of 1940 World War II was raging in Europe. Nazi Germany had just defeated France and was in control of much of the continent. Only Great Britain opposed the Nazi onslaught, and many Americans believed that the United States had to support Britain. The draft bill was one result, as were many other moves to make it easier for Britain to obtain military equipment and other supplies. After the United States finally entered World War II in December 1941, the draft was expanded. The age range was eventually broadened from eighteen to thirty-eight, and those called up had to serve for the duration of the war. Ultimately, ten million Americans were drafted in World War II.

Clifford and Spencer note how the 1940 bill made such a mass call-up responsible, and also helped garner American support for World War II policies in general. They also note that this large-scale draft did not survive the Vietnam War thirty years later as other civilians, like the original Plattsburgers, de-

J. Gary Clifford and Samuel R. Spencer Jr., from *The First Peacetime Draft*, Lawrence, KS: University Press of Kansas, 1986. Copyright © 1986 by the University Press of Kansas. All rights reserved. Reproduced by permission.

voted their attention to the issue. Clifford is a professor of political science at the University of Connecticut and is the author of The Citizen Soldiers: The Plattsburg Training Camp Movement. *Spencer is president emeritus of Davidson College and is the author of* Decision for War, 1917.

Some years after the end of World War II, [General] Lewis Hershey asked Grenville Clark [one of the authors of the 1940 draft bill] for a photograph to hang in his office at selective-service headquarters in Washington. The selective-service director thought it was only appropriate that the man who had done so much to get the draft law enacted in 1940 should be so recognized. Clark, even though he had worked closely with Hershey during the war and had developed a real fondness for the man whom most Americans thought of as "Mr. Selective Service," declined the request, saying that his own role had been "only minor."

Clark's modest assessment may have been a polite way of paying tribute to Hershey, who was to run the machinery of selective service for some thirty years, but possibly Clark's refusal more accurately reflected his own doubts about the long-term legacy of 1940. Notwithstanding his herculean efforts for selective service in 1940 and for national service after Pearl Harbor [naval base in Hawaii attacked by the Japanese on December 7, 1941, which brought the United States into World War II] the old Plattsburger [supporter of the 1940 draft bill] took up a new cause, world federalism, and became an increasingly vocal critic of American policies during the Cold War. When the Truman administration asked Congress to renew the draft in March 1948, Clark sent a wire to his old foe [Senator] Robert Taft: "Hope you will insist on much clearer evidence that war is unavoidable before approving either selective service or universal training. The assumption that Russian policy aims at world domination rather than defense against Western attack is surely not valid." Initially, Clark was concerned with the impact of the draft on what he considered an overly aggressive United States foreign policy, and his writings and backstage activities during the late 1940s and 1950s were aimed primarily at such global changes as reform of the United Nations Charter and intricate plans for nuclear disarmament. In reaction to United States involvement in Vietnam, however, the man who wrote the Burke-Wadsworth bill [the 1940 draft bill] came to be critical of the draft as an institution, particularly its channeling and deferment practices that seemed to discriminate on the basis of class and educational background. . . .

A New War and a New Era

Ironically, the draft became the most conspicuous casualty of the Vietnam War. Notwithstanding the dispatch of more than 2.5 million troops to Vietnam over the course of a decade, the United States failed to achieve its political and military goals. As casualty lists rose after 1965, political protest against the war tended to focus on the draft. Some 70 percent of the fifty-six thousand Americans who died in Vietnam were draftees. Students on college campuses burned their draft cards in symbolic protest, and Catholic priests poured blood on selective-service files in Catonsville, Maryland. Fully thirty thousand youths of draft age fled the country, while as many as half a million avoided induction through various illegal means. General Hershey, who tried to defend the system that he had administered since 1940, became the target of much vitriol. When Richard M. Nixon became president [in 1969] and began to withdraw United States forces from Vietnam, he removed Hershey from office and pledged to end the draft. In a further irony, when the Nixon administration moved to an All-Volunteer Force (AVF) in 1973, it did so by arguing that a leaner professional force that would emphasize firepower over manpower could meet all defense needs. Although the AVF would number more than two million uniformed personnel, the argument was reminiscent of the pacifist/isolationist opposition of 1940. A subtle philosophical shift also occurred, as military service was seen, not as an obligation, but as a tax. According to the presidential commission that recommended the AVF: "When not all our citizens can serve, and when only a small minority are needed, a voluntary decision to serve is the best answer, morally and practically, to the question of who should serve."

Whether or not the kind of military system that had proved so successful in two world wars should necessarily apply to the nuclear age was a question the Plattsburgers left unanswered. The political scientist Eliot A. Cohen has argued that once the United States achieved the status of a world power, it had to be prepared to fight two kinds of wars—the large conventional total wars that require full mobilization, as in 1917 and 1941, and smaller, peripheral wars and police actions that are fought with limited forces, as in Korea and Vietnam. Comparing the American experience in Korea and Vietnam with nineteenth-century Britain's small wars in Africa and Asia, Cohen contends that Anglo-Saxon countries can engage in such conflicts with greatest military success and least disruption of domestic tranquility by relying on professional forces. Yet Cohen also notes that the All-Volunteer Force, which is so dependent on superior American technology, would prove deficient in the event of a conventional war in Europe against Warsaw Pact forces. Eventually, he concludes, "demography, strategic necessity, and economic recovery will conspire to force a return to the draft. What kind of draft, however, remains as open a question as it was almost forty years ago.". . .

The army certainly profited from the Plattsburg initiative. By letting civilians lead before he took up the cudgels, General [George] Marshall [U.S. chief of staff] obtained the one mechanism necessary for raising forces that would be large enough to provide for hemispheric defense or to wage war in overseas theaters. For the remaining year of peace the army used manpower from the draft to enlarge and reorganize its structure, adapt to modern weapons and tactics, and carry out large-scale maneuvers during the summer of 1941. After Pearl Harbor, selective service permitted the army to expand enormously. Draft calls reached a peak of five hundred thousand a month by late 1942. By registering 45 million men and drafting 10 million, the system enabled the army to reach its top strength of eighty-nine divisions and 8.3 million men in 1945. More than 5 million draftees served overseas in Europe, Asia, Africa, and the Pacific, by far the most extensive war effort ever undertaken by the United States.

Even though the Plattsburg sponsors did not envisage such a large army when they introduced their bill in June 1940, they essentially planted a seed that grew in accordance with administration policy and bureaucratic blueprints. They urged the draft in 1940 on the unstated assumption that the United States should intervene in the European war on the side of Britain, but these foreign-policy desires did not dictate the outcome in 1940 or afterward. The Plattsburgers scored by getting their proposal before Congress at a crucial moment, but once it became a national issue, control slowly slipped from their hands. Just as they could not persuade the General Staff to reinstitute Plattsburg officer camps, NEC [National Emergency Committee, organization which advocated the draft] leaders could not guarantee that the draft would be used to "stand up to Hitler, et al." simply by advocating it. The waning of their influence, became evident even during the congressional debates, for it was Hershey and his aides, not Clark and [Howard C.] Petersen [one of the authors of the 1940 draft bill] who drafted the final amendments to the bill. Once selective service had passed, the NEC disbanded most of its organization, except for a small subcommittee that pushed futilely for officer training in 1941. Grenville Clark remained influential as an unofficial adviser to [Henry L.] Stimson [secretary of war] and as a founder of the interventionist Fight for Freedom Committee in 1941. Yet Clark, even as he backed lend-lease, convoys, repeal of the Neutrality Act, and other steps toward war, was always careful not to advocate publicly any premature entry into the war. His chief concern was that the United States be prepared for war if it came. As a War Department consultant, Clark helped to draft a resolution for a declaration of war on 8 December 1941, but it can hardly be said that he or the Plattsburg crowd had guided United States policy to that fateful result.

Passage of the Burke-Wadsworth bill also proved to be a turning point for the opposition. College students, as historian Justus D. Doenecke has pointed out, returned to their campuses that fall with a "certain fatalism. . . . They were not militantly interventionist but they often found isolationism futile." The peace groups in particular took their defeat as a sign that United States intervention in the war against Hitler was only a matter of time. The Committee on Militarism in Education formally dissolved itself on the fatalistic assumption that the draft had militarized all education. Pacifists redoubled their efforts at counseling conscientious objectors, and Paul French, Raymond Wilson, Roger Baldwin, and others [who opposed the draft] worked with the Selective Service System in setting up and administering Civilian Public Service Camps wherein some twelve thousand COs [conscientious objectors] who refused to do noncombatant service worked without pay during the war on projects involving reforestation, agricultural experimentation, and soil-erosion control. . . .

America in Danger

The Plattsburg effort also helped to sustain faith in American institutions at a moment of peril. Germany's sudden victories in Europe produced a crisis of confidence among Americans, a sense of despair that democratic governments could not defend against the totalitarian juggernaut. The comment by Senator [Sherman] Minton about adopting Hitlerism to defeat

Hitlerism was an extreme example. Young John F. Kennedy's slim volume *Why England Slept*, published at the height of the selective-service debate, echoed the gloomy analysis that totalitarian states that are geared to war had clear advantages over democracies, where "the cry of 'warmonger' will discourage any politician who advocates a vigorous arms policy." Nevertheless, Kennedy thought that the United States could still profit from Britain's example by getting, "our armaments *and the people behind these armaments* . . . prepared . . . even to the ultimate point of war." In the next-to-last paragraph of the book, the future president concluded: "What we need is an armed guard that will wake up when the fire first starts or, better yet, one that will not permit a fire to start at all." In a symbolic sense the old Plattsburg crowd provided the United States with such an armed guard in 1940, by writing and by lobbying through the legislation that eventually raised the military forces necessary to triumph over the Axis war machines [Germany, Japan, and Italy]. And by stressing the principle of national service and a citizen's obligation in a democracy, Clark and his colleagues articulated a rationale for military reform that harmonized with American traditions and values.

But the initiative of the Plattsburgers in 1940 has a broader implication for Americans nearly half a century later. The trauma of the Vietnam War, the end of the draft, and a nuclear arms race have diminished the links between the people, the armed forces, and the government, John Kennedy's 1940 comment that "there is no lobby for armaments" makes for quaint reading in an era when the common defense no longer seems to be the responsibility of every citizen but instead is provided by hundreds of billions of tax dollars, technical experts, and esoteric systems and strategies. But if the 1940 experience means anything, it suggests that the questions of national security are too important to be left to experts and machines. Just as the Plattsburgers and their opponents thrashed out the pros and cons of a military draft in 1940, it is still the obligation of citizens to think and debate anew the dilemmas posed by global commitments in an age when nuclear weapons can obliterate, for all time, the distinction between citizens and soldiers.

A Student for the Ministry Refuses to Register for the Draft

Donald Benedict

Many of those who resisted the draft did so out of a devotion to pacifism, a refusal to accept violence as a means of solving problems. Most twentieth century draft systems have allowed for such resistance within certain conditions. In the United States, such resisters have been generally known as conscientious objectors (COs). One's status as a CO has to be officially established by demonstrating to draft officials a pattern of religious belief or some other long-standing personal commitment to nonviolence. At that point one might be freed from service entirely or drafted into a nonviolent task.

The author of the following selection, seminary student Donald Benedict, went even further. He refused to even register for the 1940 draft, the first ever passed by the United States in peacetime. He believed that registration, followed by official CO status, would set him apart as an undeserving elite. He refused to accept this not only on the grounds of nonviolence but also because the U.S. armed forces, at that time, were officially segregated; black troops did not serve in the same units as white ones. As a result of his refusal, Benedict, as well as others in his circle, were sent to prison. The selection is from a memoir he wrote of two separate terms in prison.

Congress passed the draft registration law in July 1940. Apart from my nonviolent philosophy, how could I ever serve in a segregated army? We talked in Newark about the

Donald Benedict, from *'These Strange Criminals:' An Anthology of Prison Memoirs by Conscientious Objectors from the Great War to the Cold War*, edited by Peter Brock, Toronto, Ontario, Canada: University of Toronto Press, 2004. Copyright © University of Toronto Press, Inc. 2004. Reproduced by permission.

draft, and in September five of us decided to go on living there, continuing to work with children and identifying ourselves with workers and lay people. We rented a house and lived in a communal? Christian Ashram style, having prayers together; working at [house] painting, washing windows, and various odd jobs; putting the earnings into a common pot. Each of us took a dollar a week to spend. We decided to attend classes half-time at Union.

The draft issue quickly involved practically everyone at the seminary, where we discussed it in relation to the Christian faith. There was a minimal recognition of the legitimacy of pacifism for conscientious objectors (COs). The crux of the matter for us was that while draft registration was mandatory, seminarians were automatically exempt from military service. Certainly we did not want to be drafted into the fighting army, but neither did we want to be excused because we were different from other people or because we were members of a special class. We felt we should face the draft like anyone else, and as pacifists, we resisted involvement in the process of war.

Dal [Meredith Dallas], Dave [Dellinger] and I, living together in Newark, knew that the only consistent attitude for us was to decline to register, thereby refusing to be classed as an elite. We would be doing the same thing we did when we moved out of the seminary. Ministers, we had said, are not better than others; they are the servants. We were being protected unjustifiably. If the government's stand was based on an assumption of our pacifist beliefs, that was in error; not all seminarians were pacifists.

Another consideration was my calling to preach the gospel. I believed that it was the incarnation—the good news that God had sent his only Son, incarnate as a human being—that was central to the gospel. This identification of Jesus with all humanity made rebirth and liberation possible. Could I, as a clergyman, preaching this gospel, ever separate myself from other persons? Could I accept any kind of exemption, any favored position solely because I had indicated my intention to become a follower of Jesus? That would be ridiculous.

Finally, twenty-two of us prepared a signed statement as a public announcement of our intention to refuse to register. *The Christian Century* printed our statement; newspapers picked it up, and intense pressure was exerted—especially by our families—to get us to rescind our decision. My mother wrote that she and my father hoped I would reconsider but that they would stand by whatever decision I reached in good conscience. Their reaction was quite different from that of most others. Dave's father [a wealthy Bostonian] actually threatened suicide. It did not change Dave's mind, but other students began one by one, to succumb to the pressure. We expected opposition from "Uncle Henry" [i.e., Henry Sloane Coffin, president of Union], but we were surprised to have well-known pacifists like Harry Emerson Fosdick and Ralph Sockman, the nationally known radio preacher, come to talk to us and counsel us to register. Norman Thomas came. His brother, Evan, had been in Leavenworth during World War I for the same offense. Even the American Friends Service Committee tried to dissuade us, holding that alternative service was preferable to jail.

Pressure from All Sides

Many people misunderstood our direct purpose of course, but it was clear to me that, aside from the specific point we intended to make, the refusal to register was the most effective and concrete thing we could have done as seminary students to make public our opposition to the war and the war system.

By the time the draft law was signed—October 14, 1940—fourteen students had dropped out of our group. Some had decided to register as COs, which meant they could eventually go into Civilian Public Service (CPS). On the day we refused to register, Roger Shin left school and enlisted. He agreed with us that he ought not to have this exemption, but he thought if he believed in the war he should enlist like anyone else.

The night before the national registration day the seminary community held a public worship service as an expression of solidarity even though many students held opposing views. On the day of registration eight of us appeared before the draft board set up at the seminary and presented a signed letter stating the reasons why we, in good conscience, could not register. To our amazement, the man who took our communication was a United States district attorney. He immediately served a subpoena calling for our appearance the next day before a New York County grand jury. They handed down indictments charging us with failure to register for the draft. We pleaded guilty.

The eight of us were Dave, Dal, Howard Spragg, George Houser, Bill Lovell, Joe Bevilacqua, Dick Wichlei, and me. Ted Walsh, our lawyer, was a prominent corporation counsel who had volunteered his services. He pointed out something that had not occurred to any of us. Our joint signing of the letter indicating our intentions opened us to a possible conspiracy charge that carried a maximum sentence of forty-three years, rather than the five years maximum for draft violation. For the next month national publicity was intense. Letters came from all over the country, supporting or condemning us.

On the day of sentencing we were allowed to make a final statement to the court. Mine implied that anyone who was a Christian could take no other course. As I look back, I see that my attitude was terribly self-righteous, but at the time I was sure I was acting rightly. The judge sentenced us to a year and a day, with the stipulation that at any time we decided to register for the draft we would be immediately released. All we had to do was register, but we had found this impossible to do.

We were led out of the courtroom, handcuffed together, taken down the back elevator, and put into the paddy wagon single file. Reporters and photographers were waiting, and an Associated Press photo of the eight seminary students being taken to the federal jail at West Street was front-page news in the evening papers. Our one-week stay at West Street was an introduction to the prison system. Six of us were put in one room together and two on another floor. We were told we could write two letters during that week.

If our sole concern had been our exemption, then our logical behavior was to become model prisoners, serve the minimum term, and get out. But as pacifists, even in prison we could demonstrate against violence and racism. I tried falling into the food line for blacks only and was promptly jerked away by a guard and placed with my "own people." That night, lying awake, I heard white guards talking to prisoners, calling them "black nigger bastards."

The second day at West Street I wrote reassuringly to my mother. I had decided that stopping the war system was going to take years of hard work and long suffering, so I suggested she read up on the pacifist movement and its full implications. I told her we were kept busy doing maintenance work, but I didn't tell her what the maintenance work had been that day. Howard and I had been ordered to clean out a cell that housed drug addicts. They were men under the torture of being forced to shake their habit cold turkey. If the officials thought seminarians were squeamish, they were wrong. We would not try to avoid trouble or suffering.

CHAPTER 2

The Notion of National Service and the Military Needs of the Cold War

Chapter Preface

In the mid-1940s, World War II gave way to the Cold War, an ideological standoff between the United States and the Soviet Union as well as their respective allies. This standoff lasted until 1991. At its heart was the principle of military deterrence, or the hope that by maintaining a large military capability, one's enemy would be deterred from attacking or even thinking about attacking. Nuclear weapons played a large part in deterrence but so also did the presence of large standing armies. Countries on both sides maintained a draft through much of the Cold War. A few, Great Britain for example, only had a draft for part of that era, from 1948 to 1963. The United States maintained its peacetime draft until 1973 and then reintroduced the requirement that all young men register for Selective Service in 1980.

Cold War–era thinking about the draft was broader than earlier draft debates. Now, discussion of the draft was built upon the principle of national service, or alternatively universal military training (UMT). In UMT all young men would receive military training then remain in the reserves afterward. Many who favored UMT, such as Dwight D. Eisenhower, president of the United States from 1953 to 1961 (and a World War II general), thought that UMT would not only provide for military readiness but help contribute to solving such social problems as economic or racial divides. National service, meanwhile, might require young people to serve their countries in ways other than through military service, such as the American Peace Corps. Such forms of service might then be open to women or to those who opposed military service on nonviolent grounds.

As ever, debates over national service or UMT centered on such issues as who should serve, possible exemptions, and the balance between service and individual liberty. Few countries adopted full-blown national service, although many European nations required all young men to receive military training. In America, debates over the draft boiled over during the Vietnam War (1962–1973). In the beginning, college students and some others could get exemptions, which meant that it was mostly the poor who were drafted. Many young people simply opposed the war itself, and draft resistance was widespread. By the early 1970s, even military experts were wondering whether a volunteer army might produce a more dedicated, efficient military.

Drafting All Men Would Provide Many Benefits

Dwight D. Eisenhower

Dwight D. Eisenhower, the author of the following selection first published in 1966, carried great authority with regard to military matters and such issues as the military draft. From 1943 to 1945 he was the top allied commander in Europe, and therefore helped guide the allies to victory over Nazi Germany in World War II. From 1945 to 1948 he was chief of staff of the U.S. Army, and from 1953 to 1961, he was president of the United States.

As the selection indicates, Eisenhower was a strong supporter of universal military training for all American men, a practice already in place in many European countries. He believed that it would provide the necessary readiness for large-scale war that was always a danger during the years of the Cold War. But he also thought that it would bring many social benefits including a revived sense of patriotism and greater discipline and order. He was distressed by many of the draft exemptions, and the manipulations of those exemptions, that were common in the mid-1960s.

During the years in which I served as Chief of Staff of the Army, I tried hard but unsuccessfully to persuade Congress to establish a sound system of Universal Military Training in this country. I felt that UMT was desirable not only from the standpoint of military preparedness, but for reasons of fitness and discipline among our youth. I also believed that it would provide the fairest approach to the always thorny problem of manpower procurement.

War, of course, is always unfair to youth. Some young men have to fight and others do not, and I see no complete cure for that until the blessed day arrives when men have learned to live in peace, and there will no longer be need for military force. That day is not here, however, and it cannot come so long as an implacable enemy of human freedom strives to enslave the world. Today more than ever, therefore, I think that this country should adopt, as the cornerstone of its defense establishment, a workable plan of universal training—and I mean *universal*, with a minimum of really essential exceptions.

First, let's take a look at what our present manpower-procurement system is doing to this country.

During the past year, I have watched with dismay the rising tide of rancor engendered by our draft system. Yet it is not hard to understand why this clamorous dissent should exist. At one end of the manpower spectrum we have had the college students, who until recently were deferred almost automatically. At the other end, we have had the young men whom the military authorities deemed unfit because of physical, mental, educational or moral deficiencies. Thus, as regards military exemption, we have had two large, privileged classes.

It is from the middle of the spectrum that the Selective Service has drawn the bulk of its manpower in recent years. These are the boys who are physically fit and possess sufficient education to make good soldiers, but who for various reasons have not gone on from high school to college. With harsh irony, they refer to themselves as the "sitting ducks." They feel, and justly, that they are a highly important segment of the nation's work force and are entitled to the same consideration as our future scientists and engineers, doctors, and lawyers, professors and industrial managers.

Now, I believe implicitly the necessity of higher education for great numbers of our young people. Yet I also look back to World War II and the postwar years, and I remember vividly what happened to that generation of students. Before that conflict ended, we necessarily were taking nearly all of our able-bodied young men for military service; hundreds of thousands of college careers were delayed or interrupted. Yet when peace came, the boys who really wanted an education returned to college and in most cases finished their courses of study with a determination and maturity that were heartening to behold. Education and military service certainly are not mutually exclusive.

There have been other inequities in the draft. For several years young married men were deferred, and when our growing commitment in Vietnam necessitated increased quotas we had for a time the spectacle of many youths rushing into marriage—before they were ready to undertake the establishment of a home—in order to avoid military service. That rule is now changed. Others, by their own admission, have started fathering children as quickly as possible after marriage. This, I am told, is called "babying out."

Dubious Deferments

Many graduate schools have experienced substantial recent increases in enrollment—considerably beyond natural year-to-year growth—because some young men preferred to prolong their education rather than do their stint for their country. Deferments have also been given for so-called critical occupations, and this unquestionably has influenced some boys in the choice of careers.

All of this has resulted not only in unfairness to those young men who *are* called, but also in a state of mind which I think is very bad for America. We still have in this country, thank the Lord, a great majority of young people who do have a strong sense of patriotism, who understand and believe in the United States' effort to contain communism before it engulfs the world. But we also have a minority who use every legal loophole to avoid their obligations, who seem willing to accept the splendid opportunities that this country offers without lifting a hand to preserve our way of life. And on the outer fringe we have a few who even use deceit and other illegal means to avoid the draft. The latter should be dealt with sternly and with dispatch.

It is my hope that out of this frustrating and humiliating experience will come a better way of providing the military manpower that we must have—a system which will help revive among *all* our young people a deep sense of "duty, honor, country." It is surely one of the fundamentals of our democratic system that every young person should love and believe in his country and feel a conscientious obligation to *do something* for his country—in peace and in war. Patriotism is not only a noble emotion but an emotion that is necessary to national survival. It is also an emotion which can be diluted by bitterness engendered by a system that is deemed unfair by so many.

In hammering out any new system of manpower procurement and training, therefore, we must keep certain objectives firmly in mind:

1. It must be a system which will provide the men we must have for our worldwide commitments.

2. It must have sufficient flexibility to permit us, in times of emergency, to bring additional men into our armed forces quickly and in substantial numbers.

3. It must, as far as possible, eliminate present unfairness.

4. It should bring to every young man an understanding of his obligation to his country and a sense of participation in its affairs.

5. It should be a builder of physical fitness, self-discipline and decent personal habits.

6. It should include the vast numbers of boys who are now exempted because of educational deficiencies or moderate physical disabilities such as trick knees, overweight problems and a host of other minor and often correctable infirmities. . . .

A Year of Service for All Males

Under the system that I envision, every young male American, no matter what his status in life or his plans for the future, would spend 49 weeks—one year minus three weeks' vacation—in military training. Only the barest minimum of exemptions would be permitted: obvious mental incompetents, those with some drastic physical defect, perhaps a few extreme-hardship cases.

Basically, I have always felt that 19 is about the right age to begin military service. Boys of 19 are young enough to be flexible, and in most cases they are more mature than those of 18. There are, however, other considerations. Eighteen is usually the age at which a boy finishes high school and is ready to enter college or go to work. It is a natural break in his life. If we were to enlist boys at 18 rather than 19 or any other age, it would cause less disruption in our schools and in working careers. Therefore, all things considered, I think 18 should be the age at which our young men should begin their year of UMT.

This year should be considered not only as their contribution to country but as part of their education. The government would, of course, provide sustenance, clothing and other necessaries, but the trainees would be paid only a small stipend—say five or ten dollars a month—in order to have a bit of pocket change for incidentals.

At the beginning of the year, each UMT trainee would be offered the option of enlisting immediately in our regular forces for a two-year term of duty, with all the pay, advances and benefits pertaining thereto, including later education under the G.I. bill of rights. A great many, I believe, would choose this course.

For the large number who *remained* in UMT, the year would be spent primarily in military training. It would include regular daily stints on the training base, athletics, remedial education for those who need it, building vigorous bodies and learning the wisdom of discipline, cleanliness and good personal habits. Youngsters with correctable physical weaknesses—and we have millions of them in this favored land—would benefit from good nutrition, a year of disciplined life, and special medical attention if they needed it.

The boys in UMT could and should be used in times of emergency such as floods, storms and fires. They could be useful in helping to maintain order and in assisting the victims of misfortune. On the other hand, they should not be impressed into any regular work program outside their base. We want no semblance of forced labor in America.

Almost two million boys now reach the age of 18 each year, and in times of peace or small wars we certainly could not use that many in our regular military forces. Consequently, many of our young men would complete their period of service with the 49 weeks of UMT. They would then be free to go on to college or vocational school or to begin their careers without interruption—except in the case of a major war, when all our potential military manpower would be needed.

If the inducements of full pay and later education at government expense did not produce the volunteers that we need for our regular forces, then it would be necessary to draft the added men. To do this in the fairest way, we should employ the lottery. In the beginning, we would have to include in the lottery the large pool of youths who were past UMT age but were still liable to military service. This pool would diminish each year, and after five or six years would cease to exist. From then on, the lottery would apply only to the boys in UMT.

This basic plan is by no means original with me. I have merely selected what I regard as the best parts of many suggested plans and put them together in an integrated whole. It is impossible within the compass of a short article to fill in all the details. For example, how would we fit the R.O.T.C. [Reserve Officer Training Corps] units, the National Guard and our reserves into the UMT system? I do not believe that these worthwhile services would have to be abandoned. All such complex matters can be worked out through careful study.

A suggested variant is that we adopt a system of universal service but offer each young man the choice of military training or of serving in some civilian group such as the Peace Corps, a hospital cadre or a conservation corps. I strongly doubt the wisdom of this plan, because (1) it would be almost impossible to provide enough useful civilian duties for those who elected this course; (2) the scheme would still be unfair to the boys who have to fight our wars; (3) the important benefits of a year of military education would not reach those who chose civilian service.

I am fully aware that the plan I suggest is not perfect. There are difficulties to be surmounted in putting it into operation.

One is that there would be some disruption of normal procedures on college campuses and in vocational schools. During the first year of UMT, these institutions would have virtually no male freshman classes; the second year, few sophomores; and so on until the end of the fourth year. After that, conditions would return to normal, the only difference being that first-year college students would average a year older—which could be a good thing.

The second obstacle—and this is a tough one—is the cost. Nobody really knows the price tag of UMT, but estimates run from three to six billion dollars a year above present military expenditures. If we wished to cut the training period to six months, costs could be sharply reduced, but I think that this would also seriously dilute the benefits. In the begining, we would also have to build and equip many new military camps, thus increasing the early costs.

I have no ready-made plan for financing UMT. I wish only to say that a big, powerful country such as ours could surely find a way to pay the bill. Personally, I think the program is far more important than some of the public efforts on which we are now spending so much.

Still another problem is the procurement of training personnel—military instructors, teachers, doctors, and so on. I do not regard this problem as insurmountable. We could call in reserve officers for a time if needed, and I am confident that we could find the other necessary people if we had to—just as we did during World War II.

Opposed to these obstacles are the enormous benefits that our country would reap from such a system.

Both Military and Social Benefits

First, there are the long-term military advantages. After a few years of UMT, we would have always a huge reserve of young men with sound basic military training. The R.O.T.C. would turn out better officers; the National Guard would be far more efficient. In case of a great emergency, all these men would be ready for combat after a brief refresher course, and in the event of a nuclear attack—the Lord forbid!—a disciplined body of young men in every community would be a priceless asset.

Second, although I certainly do not contend that UMT would be a cure for juvenile delinquency, I do think it could do much to stem the growing tide of irresponsible behavior and outright crime in the United States. To expose all our young men for a year to discipline and the correct attitudes of living inevitably would straighten out a lot of potential troublemakers. In this connection—although I am sure that in saying this I label myself as old-fashioned—I deplore the beatnik [or hippie] dress, the long, unkempt hair, the dirty necks and fingernails now affected by a minority of our boys. If UMT accomplished nothing more than to produce cleanliness and decent grooming, it might be worth the price tag—and I am not altogether jesting when I say this. To me a sloppy appearance has always indicated sloppy habits of mind.

But above and beyond these advantages of UMT is the matter of attitude toward country. If a UMT system were to become a fixture of our national life, I think that resentment against military obligation would die away, that virtually every young man would take pride and satisfaction in giving a year of his life to the United States of America. After all, the good instincts lie near the surface in the young. Patriotism, a sense of duty, a feeling of obligation to country are still there. They are the noblest and the most necessary qualities of any democratic system, and I am convinced that UMT would help call them to the surface once more.

I am aware, of course, that many Congressmen regard Universal Military Training as political poison. I think they are being unduly timid. I am convinced that most Americans believe in the value of such a system, and that many others could be persuaded by an enlightened educational campaign. Most of all, I urge that we act *now*.

Universal Service Will Provide Both Individual Opportunity and Social Cohesion

Margaret Mead

In the years following the end of World War II in 1945, the debate over the military draft broadened to include the larger notion of national service requirements. In this, young people would be "drafted" into not only the armed forces but into other organizations in which they would serve their country. These included such bodies as the Peace Corps and the domestic equivalent of the Peace Corps known as Vista, and such proposed organizations as a national health corps, a national job training corps, even a national teachers corps. Young people, it was thought, might serve in these groups as an alternative to serving in the active-duty military.

In the following selection, the prominent American anthropologist Margaret Mead argues that such requirements might make for better students and citizens. Many might be granted opportunities denied them otherwise. National service, she suggests, might also provide women, half the population, with their chance to serve. Mead is the author of many books, including Male and Female *and* Coming of Age in Samoa. *She served for many years as curator of ethnology at New York's American Museum of Natural History.*

We may now turn to the other arguments in favor of universal national service. Universal national service would make it possible to assay [gauge] the defects and the potentialities of every young American on the threshold of adulthood. The tremendous disparity in schools and health conditions in different parts of the country and in different socioeconomic groups which now results in the disqualification of such large numbers, both for military service and for participation in our society, could be corrected for the whole population. Currently, the bulk of the young people so handicapped are simply rejected and left to their own devices, or left to become the subject of inadequate and prohibitively expensive programs of reeducation or rehabilitation later.

Universal service would immediately do away with the present anomalous situation in which young people with a record are exempted. The juvenile delinquent is, in a majority of cases, a type of individual who most needs reeducation and rehabilitation. Where a professional army is compromised by a large number of members with court records, a universal national service could appropriately deploy young people into service specialties which would meet many of the unfulfilled desires which had led to their encounters with the law: a love of cars, speed, and risk.

Universal registration and evaluation would also serve to find the very extensive numbers of highly talented young people whose capacities are hidden by lack of education, medical care, or social experience, or by membership in deprived ethnic and racial groups. As our civilization becomes more and more technical, the demand for talent becomes ever more intense. Our present methods of talent search are terribly inadequate.

Universal national service would provide an opportunity for young adults to establish an identity and a sense of self-respect and responsibility as individuals before making career choices or establishing homes. At present a very large number go from dependency on their parents into careers that have been chosen for them, or use early marriage as a device to reach psuedo-adult status.

Universal national service would provide an opportunity for young adults to experience the satisfaction of services performed on behalf of the nation and of other fellow citizens—children, the sick, the aged, the deprived—which could serve as a paradigm for later social participation nor immediately based on the standards of the marketplace. It should increase the capacity for dedication. Whatever methods are selected for distributing income in such a way as to separate productive ability from consumer need, universal national service could be set up as a suitable educational prelude. Universal national service, if set up in such a way that units were a cross section of the entire society, could compensate for the increasing fragmentation, ignorance, and lack of knowledge of their fellow citizens and the rest of the world which is characteristic of those reared in our economically segregated residential pattern, in which both the poor and the rich, the highly technologically gifted and those with obsolescent skills, the white collar and the blue collar, are each reared in almost total ignorance of the others.

A More Solid Society

Universal national service could be a preparation for later periods of reeducation and reevaluation which may become a necessary feature of a society faced with increasing longevity, and rapid technological change.

Universal national service could be made into a tremendous system of incentives for pupils in elementary and secondary school. If it were widely known that every child would someday have to serve in a service unit, and that his skills and abilities would give him a chance at particular kinds of service, then the incentives, which now operate for the privileged group who know they must study in order to enter college, would be extended to the whole population. The present frequency of dropouts is due not only to poor backgrounds and poor teaching, but also to lack of incentive for those young people who have, at present, no vision of higher education. Higher education as an incentive to hard work on the part of privileged American students is not wholly an academic or economic incentive; it is primarily a promise that they will be able to participate for two years, or four, or six, in the kind of life that they want to live, associate with others with the same aspirations, and find the kinds of wives they want to marry. Universal national service could extend this kind of aspiration to young people who are not capable of or interested in higher education, but who are quite capable of dreaming of living in the city instead of the country, at the seaside instead of on the plains of Kansas, who want to work near airplanes instead of at [coal] mine pitheads, or in zoos, or forestry preserves, or in something connected with science or medicine. Just as the armed services have been able to make training for a chosen but often otherwise unobtainable vocation an incentive to the recruitment of young adults, the opportunities which would he opened for choice in universal national service could be widely disseminated to the young. The hopeless, unemployed young corner boys might never reach the corner if they knew that, no matter who they were, they would have a chance, at 18, at a wider world.

Universal national service would provide for an interval within our very prolonged educational system in which actual, responsible work experience would precede further educational and vocational choices. Our present changing society demands—instead of individuals who will learn one job and, driven by the fear of hunger will stick to it all their lives— people who are flexible, able to learn new skills and perform new tasks, who will be motivated by a desire to participate in work situations rather than a simple fear of starvation. Universal national service should prepare them for this kind of participation where parents and immediate elders, who have been reared in a world of scarcity and limitation of opportunity, are not able to give them the necessary training.

Universal national service would provide opportunities for service abroad in a variety of capacities, service in different parts of the country, service in different climes and conditions. It should broaden all young people in the way in which those who have taken full advantage of service overseas and of the Peace Corps have been broadened and prepared for responsible citizenship and wider understanding of national and world problems.

The Inclusion of Women

The inclusion of women on the same basis as men is absolutely essential for the accomplishment of the goals listed above. Universal national service for men only would be so handicapped that it might be wiser to retain the present system of selective service and the present numerically few minor activities like the Peace Corps and the Job Corps. It is necessary to include women because:

Women form half of the age group involved, and a failure to include them will promote a split in the experience of men and women at a time when it is essential that they should move in step with each other, economically and politically.

The position of women today has become so identified with ideas of non-discrimination, non-segregation, and equality of privilege that failure to include women will automatically touch off latent fears of other kinds of class, race, and ethnic discrimination. The association of women with disadvantaged minorities in recent legislation, and in the thinking of many developing nations, continually reinforces this attitude. Women are not, of course, actually a minority in the same sense as racially or ethnically disadvantaged groups, and there are cogent reasons for some discrimination between the sexes but the national and world climate of opinion treats them as such.

One of the most important goals of universal national service is the identification and correction of physical and educational handicaps. These are as significant for women, as mothers of the next generation and as a large part of the labor force, as they are for men. If the women are left behind in isolated rural regions, in the slums or in ghettos, the broadening educational effects for men will be at least partially nullified because their wives will not be able to maintain the standards their husbands have learned to respect.

Universal national service will serve as a gigantic and effective talent search. Half of our intelligent and gifted citizenry are women. Because of the persistence of traditional ideas about women's aptitude, we are at present losing more highly gifted women than highly gifted men. Girls with mathematical ability are discouraged from going into the sciences or into any kind of technology they are either shunted off into typewriting or, if they persist with academic interests, into the humanities. Furthermore, it has been found that women who reenter the work force later are more likely to follow up leads which they started in college than to enter entirely new fields. The chance to assay their abilities during universal national service would provide a background for appropriate career choices when they wish to reenter the labor market and are seeking additional education.

The Vietnam-era Draft Helped Inspire Huge Protests

Jeff Leen

During the American Civil War of the 1860s, the draft resulted in huge riots in New York City. A century later, protests related to the draft flared up again. This time the protests were against the Vietnam War more generally. But many of those who participated or were sympathetic were young men who were subject to the draft or who considered the current draft laws unjust (since there were so many exemptions).

In the following selection, Washington Post *journalist Jeff Leen recalls some of the largest of these protests, which took place in Washington, D.C. The first was in 1965, followed by a "March on the Pentagon" in 1967. The last, the biggest, took place in 1971. Not long after, the United States removed its troops from Vietnam and, in a measure certainly related to both the Vietnam War and the protests against it, ended the draft.*

Metropolitan Police Lt. Robert Klotz found himself in a thin blue line of officers decked out in riot gear. In front of Klotz that November day in 1969 stood a barricade formed out of 57 city buses. Behind the buses came the constant thrum of thousands of unseen anti-war demonstrators. And behind Klotz was the White House. [President] Richard Nixon was inside, watching the Ohio State–Purdue football game on television.

As the 30-year-old Klotz stood his ground, a sergeant to his left went down in a heap. A bottle clattered to the pavement nearby.

"When you get involved in a situation where they're throwing things, you don't look straight ahead," recalled Klotz, who retired from the D.C. force as deputy chief in 1980. "You look up."

It has been a long time since D.C. police have had to master the intricacies of rock-and-bottle trajectory. But things were different in the '60s, when Washington served as a fulcrum for the forces that swirled around the divisive war in Vietnam. Every year from 1967 to 1971, a major march occurred in the District, including four of the biggest anti-war demonstrations in American history.

As the nation endured perhaps its greatest turmoil since the Civil War, Washington stood at the center, headquarters of an unpopular war, symbol of boundless power, rallying point for those who would challenge that authority. From as far as Berkeley, Calif., and as near as George Washington University they came, mainly young and bluejeaned, ardent and at times insolent for their cause.

"It was a time in which there was a very great deal of turbulence on the one hand, but also a period in which citizenship took on the form of real action," recalled Marcus Raskin, 65, a participant in many of the marches and now a public policy professor at George Washington. "It was an absolute moral choice that people took."

The orderly demonstrations of the mid-1960s snowballed into a serious attempt to shut down the government in May 1971, an occasion that set a U.S. record for people arrested in a single day.

"A lot of them came down because they felt very strongly about what they were doing," said Klotz, now 60, who worked all of the demonstrations. "And a lot of them came for adventure. And adventure meant confrontation."

The first major anti-war rally in Washington featured little confrontation. Students for a Democratic Society staged it on April 17, 1965, just one month after the United States had sent its first Marines, its first combat troops, to Vietnam. But U.S. forces there still numbered fewer than 25,000 and had not yet fought a major battle.

In that first demonstration, about 16,000 people picketed the White House and marched on the Capitol. They sang and carried earnest signs—"No More War," "We Want Peace Now." Some wore gas masks. Many wore suits and ties. Only four arrests were made.

But things were molting rapidly, as they tended to do in the '60s. The March on the Pentagon on Oct. 21, 1967, became a cultural touchstone of the decade, a defining moment of American history limned in the leonine prose of [author] Norman Mailer's Pulitzer Prize–winning *Armies of the Night*. For the first time, the counterculture openly confronted the Establishment at the seat of American power.

Opposing Both the War and the Draft

By now, 13,000 Americans had died in Vietnam and "flower power" had been loosed throughout the land from the streets of San Francisco. The draft had become a bone of contention between the generations, turning war protest into a mass effort known simply as the Movement.

The Pentagon march was the culmination of five days of nationwide anti-draft protests organized by the National Mobilization Committee to End the War in Vietnam—"the Mobe." But a singular spark was provided by the Youth International Party (Yippies), a fringe group whose leaders, Abbie Hoffman and Jerry Rubin, had announced that they planned an "exorcism" of the Pentagon. They would encircle the building, chant incantations, "levitate" the structure and drive out the evil war spirits.

The crowd drawn to Washington for the March on the Pentagon and a rally at the Lincoln Memorial numbered more than 100,000. For the first time, there were significant numbers of hippies, with long hair and fanciful garb. Hoffman donned beads and an Uncle Sam hat. Speakers included Mailer, poet Robert Lowell and pediatrician Benjamin Spock. Protest signs now brimmed with counterculture wit: "LBJ [then-president Lyndon B. Johnson], Pull Out Now, Like Your Father Should Have Done."

Mailer and Hoffman were among the 681 arrested, most for disorderly conduct and breaking police lines. More than 2,500 Army troops protected the Pentagon, which did not levitate (although Hoffman claimed to have urinated on it). Hippies pressed forward to place flowers in the barrels of soldiers' bayoneted M-14 rifles.

"Will you take my flower?" a dancing girl asked the soldiers. "Please do take my flower. Are you afraid of flowers?"

The Pentagon's steps were spattered with blood. Tear gas was unleashed on the crowds. "People became frightened," recalled Raskin, one of the speakers that day. "They began running every which way. At that moment, it turned into something else. A sense of chaos takes over."

By 1969 the Movement—now known as the "New Mobe"—had grown large enough to stage the biggest anti-war demonstration in the nation's history, the Moratorium rally on Nov. 15. More than 250,000 protesters—some estimates went as high as 500,000—poured down Pennsylvania Avenue and spilled out onto the Mall between the Capitol and the Washington Monument.

But the rancor and energy of the 1967 march seemed lacking this time. LBJ was gone. Nixon was trying to Vietnamize [turn the fighting over to the Vietnamese] the war. Big marches had lost some of their novelty.

And the government had figured out how to handle the huge crowds, monitoring the demonstration with 3,000 police officers, 9,000 Army troops (who were kept out of sight in reserve), 200 lawyers and 75 clergymen. The New Mobe had recruited thousands of its own armband-wearing "parade marshals" to help keep order.

The march was generally peaceful, except for a couple of clashes between police and demonstrators, including one led by the Yippies at the Justice Department. Police and protesters traded tear gas canisters for rocks and bottles. Windows were broken in about 50 buildings, and 135 arrests were announced.

Escalating Protests

By 1971, in the wake of Nixon's invasion of Cambodia and the killing of four students by National Guardsmen at Kent State University the year before, anger had returned to the Movement.

The intent now was to shut down the federal government by stopping the flow of traffic into the District on May Day. Klotz—by then a captain—recalled that police agents infiltrated the demonstrators, obtaining their "tactical manual" for the shutdown.

"They looked at all of the major access routes coming into the District from Maryland and Virginia, and they made assignments to demonstrators where they could go to block the streets," Klotz said. "They were going to come out in waves, so that when the first wave got arrested, the second wave would fill the streets and then a third wave and so on. They had done a pretty good job."

But Nixon had vowed to keep the city open.

"The Titanic was heading toward the iceberg," Klotz said.

The events began peacefully nearly two weeks before May Day, with more than 200,000 people attending rallies under the auspices of the National Peace Action Coalition. The Vietnam Veterans Against the War [VVAW] camped out on the Mall.

When the date for shutting down the government approached, the VVAW and most of the other protesters departed, leaving behind a hard core organized by the People's Coalition for Peace and Justice, and its more militant Mayday

Tribe. The plan was to combine massive traffic disruptions with marches on the Pentagon, the Justice Department and the Capitol over three days.

"The aim of Mayday actions is to raise the social cost of the war to a level unacceptable to America's rulers," the Mayday Tribe wrote in the tactical manual.

But after years of demonstrations, the police were ready for them.

First, they planned to make arrests on a scale never before seen. "We talked to courts to find out what was the minimum amount of information needed for an arrest," Klotz said. "How many people one person could legitimately arrest and still remember the details."

They created fill-in-the-blank field arrest forms to substitute for the standard, lengthy narratives. They equipped arrest vans with Polaroid cameras, so an officer could have his picture taken with his arrestee as a memory aid for a later court appearance. And they used a new kind of handcuffs—plastic "flexi-cuffs"—pre-numbered with badge numbers of the arresting officers.

Then they created "arrest teams"—composed of arresting officers, handcuffing officers and transporting officers, who would bring the efficiency of a production line to the task.

Finally, they launched a preemptive strike.

Before dawn on May 2, D.C. police got on a public address system and commanded 30,000 sleeping protesters to vacate West Potomac Park, the intended rallying point. People were told to leave because they were in violation of their permit. The reason: "rampant" use of drugs.

The reason was a pretext, like Capt. Louis Renault being shocked, shocked about the gambling at Rick's Cafe in [the movie] *Casablanca*. The drug use had gone on uninterrupted for days—two stations were set up to treat overdoses—but police chose to discover it just as the protesters were set to muster.

The preemptive strike worked, driving off many of the protesters. Police estimated that only 12,000 stayed around. "They were obviously somewhat bewildered," Klotz said. "When they were dispersed from the park, a lot of them just went home. It just sort of screwed up what they were going to do."

The next day, police used tear gas and mass arrests to keep the streets open. By 8 a.m., they had arrested 2,000 people, thwarting an attempt to tie up key bridges into the city. There were so many arrests that police stopped using arrest forms and simply scooped people up in vans. Lacking jail space, police held the arrestees outdoors at the Washington Redskins football practice field near Robert F. Kennedy Memorial Stadium. The day would end with more than 7,000 arrests, a record, but with surprisingly little violence—155 injuries were reported—considering the stakes.

After rush hour on Monday, May 3, Attorney General John N. Mitchell declared: "The traffic is flowing. The government is functioning."

Mayday leader Rennie Davis held his own news conference in mid-afternoon. "We want to make clear that we failed this morning to stop the U.S. government," Davis said, but he described the day's events as "almost the most major nonviolent demonstration" in the nation's history. His inarticulateness captured the surreal tenor of the moment.

To Klotz, it was just a fine piece of police work. "It was a very smart tactical maneuver. And it was carried out very well."

A few smaller protests would follow in the District but the high-water mark had been reached. The war was winding down. U.S. combat troops pulled out in 1972. The next year, the United States signed a peace treaty with North Vietnam in Paris.

No march in Washington marked the occasion.

"I don't think most people, myself included, thought [the demonstrations were] more than an existential gesture at the time," said Raskin. "But after we read the Pentagon Papers [a collection of documents that suggested the government had lied about Vietnam], it turned out the marches were very, very important in changing the direction of the war."

A Draft Resister Faces Prison

J.K. Osborne

The Vietnam War–era draft caused a great deal of controversy and social conflict, especially as the war dragged on through the late 1960s and into the 1970s. Many people thought that the draft was unfair: College students and others could get deferments or exemptions, and most of those who were drafted were poor (and disproportionately African American or Latino). Others considered the Vietnam War itself unfair or illegal, and many opposed the draft on those grounds. Still others opposed almost all war such as J.K. Osborne, the author of the following selection.

In this very personal testimonial, Osborne recalls that he was in many ways a typical young American man growing up in the 1950s and 1960s. But he came to view the military draft as immoral and opposition to it a matter of conscience. He was unable, as others did, to seek official classification as someone exempt from the draft or in a category that would not involve frontline military service. His moral commitment resulted in an eighteen-month prison sentence. After he was released, in December 1969, Osborne lived in Seattle, Washington.

My parole officer is an interesting man. He spent three years in a Japanese prisoner of war camp during the Second World War. He doesn't think what I'm doing is right.

May, at last. The month I belong to. The spring is sad this year, clouds always, and too much wind; everything seems too gray for this month of beauty. But the sun shone all day when I had my first interview with the parole officer and distracted me from what he was saying and from what I was supposed to be replying. He asked me several times if I were preoccu-

J.K. Osborne, from *I Refuse*, Philadelphia: The Westminster Press, 1971. Copyright © MCMLXXI The Westminster Press. All rights reserved. Reproduced by permission of Westminster John Knox Press.

pied with anything. Of course not—what a silly idea! How can one be preoccupied with anything when the sun is streaming through windows, a blue sky glaring down, shining flashes of light reflected off the waters of Puget Sound, all light shimmering as if alive, and all colors and smells of the plants outside the building saturating the air you breathe. No, I certainly wasn't preoccupied. But he was doing his best to distract me.

I suppose it was the day and the weather that gave me a poor impression of him. I am getting so tired of defending myself. It seems ludicrous that in a country where freedom of belief is written into its constitution, one must have to spend a good portion of one's life defending, explaining, excusing one's beliefs. I would much rather have been in my room listening to a good Russian composer than in that horribly efficient office of investigation. He sat behind his desk, trying to understand what makes me think as I do, when a good deal of the time even I don't know.

We talked for perhaps an hour and a half, or rather I did, since most of his talking was limited to questions. We discussed the Second World War, the Korean War, and the Vietnam War. We discussed offensive and defensive wars, wars of economic necessity. But I could not get him to express his own opinion as to the rightness or wrongness of any war. When we came too close to the moral question, he would resume his official capacity. Perhaps, as many people, by not judging the rightness or wrongness of war he thought he was freed from following a commitment to either belief. By letting the state settle the argument one is, in theory, freed from one's conscience. By not allowing the conscience to answer the question of right or wrong, the conscience is thereby kept "clean." Pilate [the Roman official who presided over the execution of Jesus of Nazareth] relegated his conscience to the people of the state: Was his conscience thus cleansed?

Writing My Biography

The parole officer had asked me on our first meeting to prepare for his use a short biography that would give him an idea
of my "socially acceptable" past; he wanted to know everything I had done that would speak in my favor. I found this a
difficult thing to do; I always find it difficult to beat my own
drum. But I shall include it here, exactly as it is in the official
records.

> Born June 11, 1941, Mandan, North Dakota, Katherine Bull-
> inger and Martin Osborne. Maternal grandparents first fam-
> ily to homestead in Southwestern North Dakota after emi-
> grating from Germany. Paternal grandfather share-cropper
> in Arkansas, married to American Indian. Father has been
> laborer on Northern Pacific Railroad for twenty-six years.
> Mother cooks at local school; neither parent finished el-
> ementary school. Eleven children in family; four now de-
> ceased. Extreme poverty in family until about 1958. All chil-
> dren worked to support the home. . . .
>
> Active in most high school activities: band, choir, swim-
> ming, track, student government. President of Speech Club,
> president of Drama Club, student council representative two
> years, winner of state debate tournament in 1958, editor of
> paper 1958–1959, editor of yearbook 1959, president of
> Knights of Columbus Squires Club 1958–1959, winner Elks
> Leadership Award in both 1958 and 1959, winner Elks Schol-
> arship award 1959, honored by State Rotary as one of top
> teen-agers in state in 1959, voted by classmates as most out-
> standing, 1959, voted one of twelve outstanding students by
> school faculty vote, 1959.
>
> Won a North Dakota state scholarship to Dickinson State
> College—entered fall 1959. Attended two years, was sopho-
> more class president. . . .
>
> Left Dickinson State College in 1961; according to dean of
> men subject was dissatisfied with quality of education and

his involvement in activities. Moved to Denver, took a full-time day job and went to Regis College—a private Jesuit men's college—at night, from 1961 to 1964. Graduated with honors in English, education, and social sciences, minors in philosophy and psychology. No involvement in student activities while at Regis. Refused assistantships at three leading universities to teach school in Leadville, Colorado, an economically depressed mining town.

Moved to Seattle, June, 1965, contracted with Shoreline Public Schools for junior high school teaching. According to associates, subject was going through extreme emotional crisis before resigning suddenly in December, 1965.

Traveled throughout the U.S., Canada, and Mexico, until July, 1966, when subject began work for Radio Corporation of America, Seattle branch. . . .

Enrolled in graduate school, University of Washington. Suspended from job and withdrew from school following arrest on March 8, 1968. Subject had application pending with both the Peace Corps and Volunteers in Service to America.

Writing to the Judge

I had given what information I could of myself at our second meeting, at the end of which he requested me to write a personal statement to the judge, who was hearing my case; the statement, he said, would serve as my only unofficial contact with the judge. Unofficial in that it would not be read into the court record. But again, since it is part of what has happened to me, I record it here. The letter, the biography composed by the parole officer, the results of official investigations, and the recommendations of my parole officer were bound into one file and sent to the judge. From these, and from his personal impressions, he would pass sentence on me, sometime in what I hoped would be the not-so-distant future.

Sir:

When I was much younger, and registered with the Selective Service in my hometown, I asked about being classified as a conscientious objector. I was told simply that my religion did not meet the requirements which would enable me to be classified a C.O. Recognizing this error years later, the question arises—why didn't I at a later date, apply for a C.O. classification?

In retrospect I am grateful I had been misinformed. It forced me, in the years and events that followed, to think through clearly all the possibilities of choice and the varied consequences of those choices. I was then, in a manner of speaking, forced to make a decision. Most are not as lucky as I. They are classified 4-F, or 1-Y [permanent or temporary exception on medical grounds] or any of the other categories that eliminate them from impressment [the draft]. They file away their notice with a feeling of relief, and forget about war and peace and politics to concentrate on their future.

Those who are not permanently rejected are thus left with a choice: volunteer or wait to be drafted, or pursue a course of draft-dodging. The latter is a long process but well worth the effort, as many who have succeeded know. It involves applying for temporary classifications enabling them to go to school or to work in a career labeled "vital"; getting the family doctor to write on their behalf for a physical, or mental deferment; or simply having their fathers make the right "contacts." Some father a child as quickly as possible. I do not mean to sound cynical. I know people who have done each of the above. Those who wait to be drafted or volunteer to get it over with are perhaps a bit more honorable than those seeking legal escape routes.

But all, with few exceptions, have one thing in common: They fail to see beyond the action of today to the consequences of tomorrow. Worse yet, they fail to judge the validity of their actions in the light of real moral commitment.

Those who enter the service without this commitment are nothing more than mercenaries; those who seek to escape through "legal" routes are for the most part cowards.

I began seriously considering the morality of the draft in 1964 and 1965, when this country first sent "advisers" to Vietnam and troops to the Dominican Republic. Both were obvious interferences with the internal machinations of a supposedly sovereign nation. Our mistake in the Dominican Republic was quickly recognized by members of Congress, and just as quickly covered over and forgotten for the sake of domestic tranquillity. Our mistake in Vietnam has been enlarged daily. As a teacher, more importantly as a rational human, I could not ignore these events, leaving the decisions up to those who were in position to "know more than we do" about the situations. I had to make a decision for myself.

The United States is my home, my country, my birthplace; I am rooted here; it has my total allegiance. Had it not, I would long ago have left. But when we love someone, we give of ourselves to help that person achieve his greatest potential. It must be the same if we love the country we live in. We must give of ourselves to help America find its true greatness. For this reason, and this alone, I have not applied for a reclassification. Impressment under any conditions is wrong; impressment during years of peace in order to "keep the peace" is totally repugnant to the ideal of a peace-loving society, and is a self-inherent contradiction. Because impressment is undemocratic, against the principles of freedom, I must do all I can to try to make it unlawful, to try to take it away from the "ideal" America.

So it was that in early 1967, after two years of great concern, I chose to make my commitment. I have had doubts throughout this period, but deep questioning always leads me to the same answer. Even at this time it is possible for me to reverse my decision and live "within the law." It is not the spirit of law which I rebel against; it is the philosophy behind this particular law which my conscience insists is wrong. To take no action would be worse than breaking that law. To live within an evil law is to live within evil. This I am not able to do, so long as I have a mind to reason, a heart to feel, and a spirit to believe.

THE
HISTORY
OF
ISSUES

The Military Draft, Citizenship, and Personal Freedom

Chapter Preface

In the United States the recurrent theme of draft debates is the extent to which a draft violates the ideal of individual freedom. During America's early years, attempts to impose a draft were fought off with claims that a draft might place undue demands on one's liberty, and that it might even constitute a form of slavery.

These objections largely held until the country needed a large army. America's first large-scale draft with few exemptions came during World War I. Its 1917 draft law faced many legal challenges, but the U.S. Supreme Court finally decided that the government had the right to enact a draft since the Constitution gives it the right to wage wars and raise armies. This decision negated all future legal challenges that were based on the principle of the violation of individual liberty. In later drafts, even those who opposed the use of violence on religious grounds had to register and then establish themselves as conscientious objectors (COs). During the Vietnam War, U.S. courts even declared that the burning of draft cards as a symbolic protest was not a form of protected free speech. Those who did so could be prosecuted, just as those who "dodged" the draft entirely might be.

Throughout, intellectuals and observers debated the justifications for and the desirable types of a draft. Some continued to wonder whether a draft was culturally as well as militarily desirable. And if that was the case, others thought, why not consider drafting women as well? They enjoyed the same citizenship status as men. Why should they not face the same obligations?

The U.S. Supreme Court Establishes That the Draft Is Constitutional

Edward D. White

The following selection is from an opinion issued by the U.S. Supreme Court in January 1918. The Court was ruling on a number of challenges to the Selective Service Act passed by the government when the United States entered World War I in 1917. This act was the most comprehensive draft law yet passed in America. It required all men between the ages of eighteen and thirty-five to register. Some twenty-four million did and, of those, nearly three million were drafted.

The 1917 act was challenged on numerous grounds. Some claimed that the draft amounted to "involuntary servitude" and was therefore unconstitutional. Others challenged it on the basis of religious belief, or on the previous examples in American history of the states, rather than the national government, being able to raise armies. But Chief Justice Edward D. White, speaking for the majority of the Supreme Court, held that as long as Congress has the right to wage war, it has the right to summon national armies. This decision set a precedent against which future challenges to the draft are judged.

We are here concerned with some of the provisions of the Act of May 18, 1917, entitled, "An Act to authorize the President to increase temporarily the Military Establishment of the United States." The law, as its opening sentence declares, was intended to supply temporarily the increased military force which was required by the existing emergency, the war then and now flagrant. The clause we must pass upon and those which will throw light on their significance are briefly summarized:

Edward D. White, *The Selective Draft Law Cases*, 245 U.S. 375–390, 1918.

The act proposed to raise a national army, first, by increasing the regular force to its maximum strength and there maintaining it; second, by incorporating into such army the members of the National Guard and National Guard Reserve already in the service of the United States (Act of Congress of June 3, 1916), and maintaining their organizations to their full strength; third, by giving the President power in his discretion to organize by volunteer enlistment four divisions of infantry; fourth, by subjecting all male citizens between the ages of twenty-one and thirty to duty in the national army for the period of the existing emergency after the proclamation of the President announcing the necessity for their service; and fifth, by providing for selecting from the body so called, on the further proclamation of the President, 500,000 enlisted men, and a second body of the same number should the President in his discretion deem it necessary. To carry out its purposes the act made it the duty of those liable to the call to present themselves for registration on the proclamation of the President so as to subject themselves to the terms of the act and provided full federal means for carrying out the selective draft. It gave the President in his discretion power to create local boards to consider claims for exemption for physical disability or otherwise made by those called. The act exempted from subjection to the draft designated United States and state officials as well as those already in the military or naval service of the United States, regular or duly ordained ministers of religion and theological students under the conditions provided for, and, while relieving from military service in the strict sense the members of religious sects as enumerated whose tenets excluded the moral right to engage in war, nevertheless subjected such persons to the performance of service of a non-combatant character to be defined by the President.

The proclamation of the President calling the persons designated within the ages described in the statute was made, and the plaintiffs in error, who were in the class and under the statute were obliged to present themselves for registration and subject themselves to the law, failed to do so and were prosecuted under the statute for the penalties for which it provided. They all defended by denying that there had been conferred by the Constitution upon Congress the power to compel military service by a selective draft, and asserted that even if such power had been given by the Constitution to Congress, the terms of the particular act for various reasons caused it to be beyond the power and repugnant to the Constitution. The cases are here for review because of the constitutional questions thus raised, convictions having resulted from instructions of the courts that the legal defenses were without merit and that the statute was constitutional.

Congress Can Raise Armies

The possession of authority to enact the statute must be found in the clauses of the Constitution giving Congress power "to declare war . . . to raise and support armies, but no appropriation of money to that use shall be for a longer term than two years . . . to make rules for the government and regulation of the land and naval forces." And of course the powers conferred by these provisions like all other powers given carry with them as provided by the Constitution the authority "to make all laws which shall be necessary and proper for carrying into execution the foregoing powers."

As the mind cannot conceive an army without the men to compose it, on the face of the Constitution the objection that it does not give power to provide for such men would seem to be too frivolous for further notice. It is said, however, that since under the Constitution as originally framed state citizenship was primary and United States citizenship but derivative and dependent thereon, therefore the power conferred upon Congress to raise armies was only coterminous with United States citizenship and could not be exerted so as to cause that citizenship to lose its dependent character and dominate state citizenship. But the proposition simply denies to Congress the power to raise armies which the Constitution gives. That power by the very terms of the Constitution, being delegated, is supreme. In truth the contention simply assails the wisdom of the framers of the Constitution in conferring authority on Congress and in not retaining it as it was under the Confederation in the several States. Further it is said, the right to provide is not denied by calling for volunteer enlistments, but it does not and cannot include the power to exact enforced military duty by the citizen. This however but challenges the existence of all power, for a governmental power which has no sanction to it and which therefore can only be exercised provided the citizen consents to its exertion is in no substantial sense a power. It is argued, however, that although this is abstractly true, it is not concretely so because as compelled military service is repugnant to a free government and in conflict with all the great guarantees of the Constitution as to individual liberty, it must be assumed that the authority to raise armies was intended to be limited to the right to call an army into existence counting alone upon the willingness of the citizen to do his duty in time of public need, that is, in time of war. But the premise of this proposition is so devoid of foundation that it leaves not even a shadow of ground upon which to base the conclusion. Let us see if this is not at once demonstrable. It may not be doubted that the very conception of a just government and its duty to the citizen includes the reciprocal obligation of the citizen to render military service in case of need and the right to compel it. To do more than state the proposition is absolutely unnecessary in view of the practical illustration afforded by the almost universal legislation to that effect now in force. In England it is certain that before the Norman Conquest [in 1066] the duty of the great militant body of the citizens was recognized and enforcible. It is unnecessary to follow the long controversy between Crown and Parliament as to the branch of the government in which the power resided, since there never was any doubt that it somewhere resided. So also it is wholly unnecessary to explore the situation for the purpose of fixing the sources whence in England it came to be understood that the citizen or the force organized from the militia as such could not without their consent be compelled to render service in a foreign country, since there is no room to contend that such principle ever rested upon any challenge of the right of Parliament to impose compulsory duty wherever the public exigency exacted, whether at home or abroad. This is exemplified by the present English Service Act.

Many Precedents

In the [American] Colonies before the separation from England [in 1776] there cannot be the slightest doubt that the right to enforce military service was unquestioned and that practical effect was given to the power in many cases. Indeed the brief of the Government contains a list of Colonial acts manifesting the power and its enforcement in more than two hundred cases. And this exact situation existed also after the separation. Under the Articles of Confederation [the first attempt at a constitution in 1776] it is true Congress had no such power, as its authority was absolutely limited to making calls upon the States for the military forces needed to create and maintain the army, each State being bound for its quota as called. But it is indisputable that the States in response to the calls made upon them met the situation when they deemed it necessary by directing enforced military service on the part of the citizens. In fact the duty of the citizen to render military service and the power to compel him against his consent to do so was expressly sanctioned by the constitutions of at least nine of the States, an illustration being afforded by the following provision of the Pennsylvania constitution of 1776. "That every member of society hath a right to be protected in the enjoyment of life, liberty, and property, and therefore is bound to contribute his proportion towards the expense of that protection, and yield his personal service when necessary, or an equivalent thereto." While it is true that the States were sometimes slow in exerting the power in order to fill their quotas—a condition shown by resolutions of Congress calling upon them to comply by exerting their compulsory power to draft and by earnest requests by Washington to Congress that a demand be made upon the States to resort to drafts to fill their quotas—that fact serves to demonstrate instead of to challenge the existence of the authority. A default in exercising a duty may not be resorted to as a reason for denying its existence.

When the Constitution came to be formed it may not be disputed that one of the recognized necessities for its adoption was the want of power in Congress to raise an army and the dependence upon the States for their quotas. In supplying the power it was manifestly intended to give it all and leave none to the States, since besides the delegation to Congress of authority to raise armies the Constitution prohibited the States, without the consent of Congress, from keeping troops in time of peace or engaging in war.

To argue that as the state authority over the militia prior to the Constitution embraced every citizen, the right of Congress to raise an army should not be considered as granting authority to compel the citizen's service in the army, is but to express in a different form the denial of the right to call any citizen to the army. Nor is this met by saying that it does not exclude the right of Congress to organize an army by voluntary enlistments, that is, by the consent of the citizens, for if the proposition be true, the right of the citizen to give consent would be controlled by the same prohibition which would deprive Congress of the right to compel unless it can be said that although Congress had not the right to call because of state authority, the citizen had a right to obey the call and set aside state authority if he pleased to do so. And a like conclusion demonstrates the want of foundation for the contention that, although it be within the power to call the citizen into the army without his consent, the army into which he enters after the call is to be limited in some respects to services for which the militia it is assumed may only be used, since this admits the appropriateness of the call to military service in the army and the power to make it and yet destroys the purpose for which the call is authorized—the raising of armies to be under the control of the United States.

Conscription Can Help Release Powerful Qualities Outside of Military Needs

William James

The following selection was written by the renowned American philosopher William James and first published in 1912. By that year many European powers, as well as Japan, had adopted conscription as a means to build truly national armies, although the United States had dropped the draft after the Civil War of the 1860s.

James was in favor of peaceful relations between nations, and he feared the growth of unchecked national armies and advanced weapons technology. But he also believed, as the selection suggests, in conscription. He thought that it would provide greater social discipline as well as give a sense of vigor and purpose to those whose working lives lacked it. He admired what he considered military "virtues," but thought they might best be put to use outside of destructive warfare.

I will now confess my own utopia. I devoutly believe in the reign of peace and in the gradual advent of some sort of a socialistic equilibrium. The fatalistic view of the war-function is to me nonsense, for I know that war-making is due to definite motives and subject to prudential checks and reasonable criticisms, just like any other form of enterprise. And when whole nations are the armies, and the science of destruction vies in intellectual refinement with the sciences of production, I see that war becomes absurd and impossible from its own monstrosity. Extravagant ambitions will have to be replaced by reasonable claims, and nations must make common cause

William James, "The Moral Equivalent of War," *The Writings of William James*, edited by John J. McDermott, New York: Modern Library, 1968.

against them. I see no reason why all this should not apply to yellow as well as to white countries, and I look forward to a future when acts of war shall be formally outlawed as between civilized peoples.

All these beliefs of mine put me squarely into the anti-militarist party. But I do not believe that peace either ought to be or will be permanent on this globe, unless the states pacifically organized preserve some of the old elements of army-discipline. A permanently successful peace-economy cannot be a simple pleasure-economy. In the more or less socialistic future towards which mankind seems drifting we must still subject ourselves collectively to those severities which answer to our real position upon this only partly hospitable globe. We must make new energies and hardihoods continue the manliness to which the military mind so faithfully clings. Martial virtues must be the enduring cement; intrepidity, contempt of softness, surrender of private interest, obedience to command, must still remain the rock upon which states are built—unless, indeed, we wish for dangerous reactions against commonwealths fit only for contempt, and liable to invite attack whenever a centre of crystallization for military-minded enterprise gets formed anywhere in their neighborhood.

Military Values Are Good

The war-party is assuredly right in affirming and reaffirming that the martial virtues, although originally gained by the race through war, are absolute and permanent human goods. Patriotic pride and ambition in their military form are, after all, only specifications of a more general competitive passion. They are its first form, but that is no reason for supposing them to be its last form. Men now are proud of belonging to a conquering nation, and without a murmur they lay down their persons and their wealth, if by so doing they may fend off subjection. But who can be sure that *other aspects of one's country* may not, with time and education and suggestion enough, come to be regarded with similarly effective feelings of pride and shame? Why should men not some day feel that it is worth a blood-tax to belong to a collectivity superior in *any* ideal respect? Why should they not blush with indignant shame if the community that owns them is vile in any way whatsoever? Individuals, daily more numerous, now feel this civic passion. It is only a question of blowing on the spark till the whole population gets incandescent, and on the ruins of the old morals of military honor, a stable system of morals of civic honor builds itself up. What the whole community comes to believe in grasps the individual as in a vise. The war-function has grasped us so far; but constructive interests may some day seem no less imperative, and impose on the individual a hardly lighter burden.

Let me illustrate my idea more concretely. There is nothing to make one indignant in the mere fact that life is hard, that men should toil and suffer pain. The planetary conditions once for all are such, and we can stand it. But that so many men, by mere accidents of birth and opportunity, should have a life of *nothing else* but toil and pain and hardness and inferiority imposed upon them, should have *no* vacation, while others natively no more deserving never get any taste of this campaigning life at all,—*this* is capable of arousing indignation in reflective minds. It may end by seeming shameful to all of us that some of us have nothing but campaigning, and others nothing but unmanly ease. If now—and this is my idea—there were, instead of military conscription a conscription of the whole youthful population to form for a certain number of years a part of the army enlisted against *Nature*, the injustice would tend to be evened out, and numerous other goods to the commonwealth would follow. The military ideals of hardihood and discipline would be wrought into the growing fibre of the people; no one would remain blind as the luxurious classes now are blind, to man's relations to the globe he lives on, and to the permanently sour and hard foundations of his higher life. To coal and iron mines, to freight trains, to fishing fleets in December, to dish-washing, clothes-washing, and window-washing, to road-building and tunnel-making, to foundries and stoke-holes, and to the frames of sky-scrapers, would our gilded youths be drafted off, according to their choice, to get the childishness knocked out of them, and to come back into society with healthier sympathies and soberer ideas. They would have paid their blood-tax, done their own part in the immemorial human warfare against nature; they would tread the earth more proudly, the women would value them more highly, they would be better fathers and teachers of the following generation.

Conscription for Everyone

Such a conscription, with the state of public opinion that would have required it, and the many moral fruits it would bear, would preserve in the midst of a pacific civilization the manly virtues which the military party is so afraid of seeing disappear in peace. We should get toughness without callousness, authority with as little criminal cruelty as possible, and painful work done cheerily because the duty is temporary, and threatens not, as now, to degrade the whole remainder of one's life. I spoke of the "moral equivalent" of war. So far, war has been the only force that can discipline a whole community, and until an equivalent discipline is organized, I believe that war must have its way. But I have no serious doubt that the ordinary prides and shames of social man, once developed to a certain intensity, are capable of organizing such a moral equivalent as I have sketched, or some other just as effective for preserving manliness of type. It is but a question of time, of skillful propagandism, and of opinion-making men seizing historic opportunities.

The martial type of character can be bred without war. Strenuous honor and disinterestedness abound elsewhere. Priests and medical men are in a fashion educated to it, and we should all feel some degree of it imperative if we were conscious of our work as an obligatory service to the state. We should be *owned* as soldiers are by the army, and our pride would rise accordingly. We could be poor, then, without humiliation, as army officers now are. The only thing needed hence-forward is to inflame the civic temper as past history has inflamed the military temper. [British author] H.G. Wells, as usual, sees the centre of the situation. "In many ways," he says, "military organization is the most peaceful of activities. When the contemporary man steps from the street, of clamorous insincere advertisement, push, adulteration, underselling and intermittent employment into the barrack-yard, he steps on to a higher social plane, into an atmosphere of service and cooperation and of infinitely more honorable emulations. Here at least men are not flung out of employment to degenerate because there is no immediate work for them to do. They are fed and drilled and trained for better services. Here at least a man is supposed to win promotion by self-forgetfulness and not by self-seeking. And beside the feeble and irregular endowment of research by commercialism, its little short-sighted snatches at profit by innovation and scientific economy, see how remarkable is the steady and rapid development of method and appliances in naval and military affairs! Nothing is more striking than to compare the progress of civil conveniences which has been left almost entirely to the trader, to the progress in military apparatus during the last few decades. The house-appliances of to-day for example, are little better than they were fifty years ago. A house of to-day is still almost as ill-ventilated, badly heated by wasteful fires, clumsily arranged and furnished as the house of 1858. Houses a couple of hundred years old are still satisfactory places of residence, so little have our standards risen. But the rifle or battleship of fifty years ago was beyond all comparison inferior to those we possess; in power, in speed, in convenience alike. No one has a use now for such superannuated [old and obsolete] things."

Wells adds that he thinks that the conceptions of order and discipline, the tradition of service and devotion, of physical fitness, unstinted exertion, and universal responsibility, which universal military duty is now teaching European nations, will remain a permanent acquisition, when the last ammunition has been used in the fireworks that celebrate the final peace. I believe as he does. It would be simply preposterous if the only force that could work ideals of honor and standards of efficiency into English or American natures should be the fear of being killed by the Germans or the Japanese. Great indeed is Fear; but it is not, as our military enthusiasts believe and try to make us believe, the only stimulus known for awakening the higher ranges of men's spiritual energy.

Many of the Alleged Benefits of a Draft Are Questionable

James C. Miller III

In the following selection, economist James C. Miller III takes issue with those who claim that a military draft provides such social benefits as greater patriotism and a sense of democracy. On the contrary, he suggests, a draft might only produce greater social conflict or thoughtless, perhaps dangerous, enthusiasm for the military.

Miller wrote the article from which the selection comes in 1968. Then, the United States was embroiled in a war in Vietnam that many had ceased believing in, and there were widespread protests against the draft. Over the next years, and despite the fact that changes were made in the draft procedures to make them fairer, America's drafted army became less disciplined and, perhaps, less effective. The draft ended in 1973 and the United States shifted to what Miller preferred: an all-volunteer army. Miller taught at the University of Virginia before becoming a scholar at the American Enterprise Institute. He served as President Ronald Reagan's budget director from 1985 to 1988.

The primary function of Selective Service is to provide manpower for national defense, but it is very often argued by advocates of conscription that military service is desirable in its own right, that it instills in the recruit a love of country and democratic ideals and offers him the opportunity of rectifying health and educational deficiencies. Because of this, they argue, military service should be expanded to include more of our youth, especially those who need such training most. . . .

James C. Miller III, "Nonmilitary Reasons for Military Conscription," *Why the Draft? The Case for a Volunteer Army*, New York, NY: Penguin Books, Inc., 1968. Copyright © 1968 by James C. Miller III. Used by permission of Penguin Group (USA) Inc.

Does Military Service Improve the Recruit?

Principal among the arguments that military training is desirable in and of itself is that military service instills in recruits democratic ideals. Witness the following quotation from Lieutenant General William Knudsen:

> A period of one year in the service of the State or of the Government will make men more democratic. They will all be together. They will learn each other's ways and learn to look upon the nation as a whole. They will be more patriotic when they get through with their service, and they will never forget the time that they had working for their country.[1]

While it is true that few ex-servicemen will ever forget the time that they had in service, whether they remember it with pleasure or consider it a wasted time in their lives depends in most cases on whether they joined voluntarily or were driven into service under compulsion.

Firstly, let us meet the rather naive notion that men learn democracy by living it in the military. Are things done in the services by group decision or by dictate from above? Unless things have changed radically in the last few months, seldom, if ever, does the recruit have any voice in what he does or how he does it. He is told what to do by a sergeant, who is told by a lieutenant, who is, in turn, told by someone else. In our whole society there is probably no more an authoritarian group than the military services. Yet some would have us believe that service in such a group teaches men to be democratic. Perhaps this is true, but only because men realize the value of individual freedom after losing it for a while.

Life in the military is said to teach young men how to cooperate with each other; how to get things done together. And in the process, innate biases and prejudices are erased. Jew and Gentile, Protestant and Catholic, Negro and white: all live and work together. The amalgamation generates understanding and tolerance on the part of soldiers which they retain after leaving the service. But it is not at all certain that recruits always lose prejudices in the military. In fact, they often gain prejudices where none existed before. Since soldiers have no choice of their fellow squad members, there is likely to be more social friction than where men are allowed to choose their own companions. And in any case, whatever the advantages of the military, they are of much less importance now than in the past, for the wider knowledge, mobility, and tolerance of today's youth render such alleged social advantages marginal.

What advocates of conscription really seem to have in mind is not that military service teaches the recruit democratic processes, but that it teaches him patriotism and love of country. For instance, the American Legion [a pro-military organization] maintains an official position that our nation should never be without an obligation for every youth to serve his country in a military capacity. . . .[2] Former President Eisenhower reported that . . . above and beyond all . . . [the] . . . advantages of universal military training is the matter of attitude toward country.[3] And, according to Senator Strom Thurmond, Military service would teach these young people patriotism and love of country and respect of the flag and discipline.[4] It is true that the vast majority of ex-servicemen consider themselves more patriotic now than when they entered the service. Military service usually does instill in the recruit a sense of pride in his country, and if the majority of Americans want these feelings taught to their youth, then military service is certainly one way to do it.

There is another argument on behalf of military training that does not stand up as well. Recruits, it is said, enter the service with sloppy physical and mental habits, but leave it strong of character and sound in mind and body. General Eisenhower reported that if UMT [universal military training] accomplished nothing more than to produce cleanliness and decent grooming, it might be worth the price tag. To me, a sloppy appearance has always indicated sloppy habits of mind.[5] Senator Thurmond expressed the same notion when he said that conscription would give them an opportunity to learn a lot in the service; and it would also give an opportunity for them to be examined physically and have any defects corrected, including dental work.[6] For those who have serious mental and physical deficiencies but meet minimum standards for military service, such problems are often corrected. Whether military service encourages good habits where none existed before is another matter. For most recruits, the language used by the drill sergeant is, by far, more foul than anything they would have heard in civilian life. Since these men are looked up to and obeyed, it is only natural that the recruit adopts the same bad habit. The entire 70-man platoon learns to keep the latrine clean by using a single toilet. Other, similar examples could be cited, but these serve to suggest that some good habits are learned, but some bad ones are learned also.

Another character argument is that the military is said to teach the recruit obedience and discipline. Obedience to one's superiors is a fundamental law of military service, but what relevance such training has to civilian life after service is somewhat in doubt. Obedience to whom? To whom is the recruit obedient in civilian life? It is said, of course, that many enter the services without respect for law and order, and that military training remedies such deficiencies. But the very ones who need such remedies most are never accepted for service—even if they volunteer. The military does not want juvenile delinquents in its ranks; besides, such training can be given best by other institutions. Discipline is forced upon the recruit where possible, but there is evidence that the long-run effects are just the opposite. The recruit learns that he should never volunteer for anything, and that the less he can get away with doing, the better off he is. This evasion mentality is the source of the term gold brick and doubtless has serious effects on the recruit's attitudes toward civilian employment after he leaves the military.

Military service is also said to mature a young person. Many college officials remember the seriousness with which veterans of World War II and Korea applied themselves to college work, and they now wish for the same attitude on the part of today's students. Many parents have sent their boy off to the army to have him return a man. The simple fact is that service in the military takes time, and men are older when they leave service than when they entered. Whether the typical 22-year-old ex-serviceman is more mature than he would have been without military service is a question open to considerable discussion.

Closely aligned with these arguments that military service is society's benefactor is the contention that the imposition of conscription and selective deferments channels youths into the roles that society considers of greatest importance. The doctrine has been stated plainly by Selective Service Headquarters:

> Delivery of manpower for induction into the armed forces has become in some respects a collateral by-product of the Selective Service System operation.... The process of channeling manpower by deferment is entitled to much credit for the large number of graduate students in the technical fields and for the fact that there is not a greater shortage of teachers, engineers, and other scientists working in activities which are essential to the national defense.[7]

The threat of induction and the use of selective deferments does "channel" men into actions they would not have taken otherwise. But these include premature marriages, "planned" children, and packing colleges with nonstudents seeking to avoid induction.

Even if we conclude that military training and the threat of the draft do tend to generate patriotism and channel youths into occupations which society feels are somehow better than those they would have otherwise chosen, there are offsetting-

disadvantages. Even if it were admitted that, on balance, military service somehow improves the recruit, it may not be worth the cost. . . .

Freedom, Justice, and Democratic Ideals

Whatever the nonmilitary advantages of conscription in excess of its costs, we must make clear that these advantages accrue to someone other than the conscripted recruit. If this were not so, then the system would not involve conscription at all, but would be an all-volunteer service. If every recruit considered the advantages accruing to him to outweigh the costs he would forgo, then he would rationally choose to volunteer for military training. The fact is that conscription *forces* youths into service. Under these circumstances such terms as privilege of service have no meaning, for a privilege is an alternative one might choose voluntarily. By definition, no one who is forced into service could ever consider such service a privilege.

In fact, an attitude exactly opposite from our tradition of freedom, equity, and individual rights was displayed by Director of Selective Service, General [Lewis] Hershey, in testimony before a House Committee in July 1966:

> I do not want to go along with a volunteer basis. I think a fellow should be compelled to become better and not let him use his discretion whether he wants to get smarter, more healthy or more honest. . . .[8]

Why is it that we want to take grown men—some who can vote and some who cannot—and force them to give up two or more years of their personal plans, ambitions, and chosen vocations—allegedly for their own good? As Senator Mark Hatfield, replied to the words of General Hershey quoted above, That is not the American way. That sounds like Russia.[9]

One problem that every patriot wrestles with is the danger of becoming too zealous in support of the military. Note the following quotation:

The army trained men for unconditional responsibility at a time when this quality had grown rare and evasion of it was becoming more and more the order of the day . . . ; it trained men in personal courage in an age when cowardice threatened to become a raging disease and the spirit of sacrifice, the willingness to give oneself for the general welfare, was looked on almost as stupidity, and the only man regarded as intelligent was the one who best knew how to indulge and advance his own ego. . . . The army trained men in idealism and devotion to the fatherland and its greatness while everywhere else greed and materialism had spread abroad.[10]

The words are those of Adolf Hitler. Note the parallel between this statement and those occasionally made by our nation's political and military leaders, not to throw suspicion on their intentions but to see how narrow is the line between patriotism and misguided nationalism. As if he were writing just to support, by implication, the thesis of this book, Hitler, after lavishing praise upon the army, goes on to say, *perhaps its sole mistakes was the institution of voluntary one-year enlistment.* Now simply because an adversary advocates one thing does not necessarily mean that we should adopt the opposite, else the leaders of the Soviet Union, North Vietnam, and Red China [totalitarian communist states] need only advocate a continuation of U.S. defense policy for them to accomplish the reverse. But what Hitler does say about voluntary enlistment suggests that this is one of the most potent weapons we have for assuring that our feelings of patriotism never transgress over into blind nationalism.

Our nation's heritage has been one of individual rights, justice, and democratic ideals. There is much danger in conscription of abridging these goals. There are both advantages and disadvantages to military service, and the best way to discover the net effects is to allow the potential recruit to decide for himself. This principle of allowing people to choose voluntarily the occupation they wish to pursue is the most compatible with our heritage. The most fundamental principle in

129

our Constitution regarding the maintaining of military forces is that all such forces should be under civilian control and civilian direction. Since conscription involves excessive use of military forces, there is far more danger that this principle will be abridged through conscription than through its conceptual opposite, a volunteer army.

Endnotes

1. Statement before House Committee on Military Affairs, Nov. 27, 1945.

2. Statement by William C. Doyle, Chairman, National Security Commission, American Legion, testifying before the Senate Committee on Armed Services, March 12, 1963.

3. Dwight D. Eisenhower, "This Country Needs Universal Miltary Training," *Reader's Digest* (Sep. 1966) p. 55.

4. Senator Strom Thurmond, *The Cavalier Daily* (March 29, 1967) p. 1.

5. Dwight D. Eisenhower, *ibid.*

6. Strom Thurmond, *ibid.*

7. "Channeling," Field Division, National Headquarters, Selective Service System, 1960.

8. Quoted in Senator Mark O. Hatfield's "The Draft Should be Abolished," *Saturday Evening Post* (July 1, 1967) p. 12.

9. *Ibid.*

10. Adolf Hitler, *Mein Kampf* (Boston: Houghton Mifflin Co. 1943) p. 280. This quotation was pointed out in James Powell's excellent article, "Anti-Militarism and Laissez Faire," *New Individualist Review*, IV, No. 4 (Spring 1967) p. 38.

The Reasons American Women Have Not Been Drafted Are Changing

M.C. Devilbiss

In the following selection, sociologist M.C. Devilbiss examines the many reasons why American women have never been drafted despite the fact that they have served in or supported the armed forces in many ways, including armed combat. These reasons are wide-ranging, and include the nature of warfare as well as assumptions about proper gender roles. Devilbiss also notes that, in earlier periods of American history, women were not considered full citizens and therefore not subject to the same kinds of citizenship obligations that men faced.

In the world of the 1980s and after, as Devilbiss suggests, the question of women and the draft is changing. New forms of combat and military technology, an emphasis on negotiation as opposed to warfare, and changing gender roles might keep the issue very much alive. M.C. Devilbiss served in the U.S. Army as well as in the Air National Guard. She has a PhD in sociology from Purdue University.

Whereas women have been utilized by the U.S. military, they have not as a class been *conscripted*. Why? We can construct some answers to this question by first analyzing five major points.

Concepts of Defense and of International Relations Are Changing

For most of its preindustrial history, the United States relied on a strategy of defensive domestic retaliation. Wars were

M.C. Devilbiss, "Women and the Draft," *The Military Draft: Selected Readings on Conscription*, edited by Martin Anderson, Stanford, CA: Hoover Institution Press, 1982. Copyright © 1982 by the Board of Trustees of the Leland Stanford Junior University. Reprinted by permission.

fought principally on domestic lands and waters, and armies and navies were typically small, localized forces. So it was relatively easy for women to take part in and with the uniformed forces, although the exact extent of their participation and the roles they assumed were dictated largely by the perceptions of those who were in charge (men) and the concept of military need, variously defined.

With the advent of industrialization, however, military strategy concepts and international relationships altered dramatically. Many Americans were forced to think in more macroscopic [wider] terms. Defense could no longer be restricted to the home front or conceptualized as a localized boundary. Through many technological advances, the world had gotten smaller. Now defense was a global issue. The small, localized armed forces of the past gave way to large, standing military forces and the perceived need for a global presence. If there were more personnel spaces available in the military and not enough qualified men to fill them, women could be looked to as an important alternative source of supply. But this could occur only if military roles could be legitimated for women. This indeed did happen because [along] with the change in concepts of defense/international relations, there was a change in the structure of the military organization.

The Structure of the Military Is Changing

The rise of industrialization in the twentieth century created drastic changes in the military as an organization. It became larger, more differentiated, and increasingly complex, as did many other social institutions at the time. The modern military required new, more, and different kinds of jobs. Whereas the military forces of the eighteenth and nineteenth centuries were made up primarily of persons with combat jobs, those of the twentieth century came to be composed largely of persons in support, service, and *non*combat specialties. This is referred to as a change in the "tooth-to-tail ratio." And it relates to the idea of "allowing" women to fight: If women cannot or are not permitted to fight, there is little room for them in a military organization in which most jobs involve fighting; but if most jobs in a military organization are those which women can do or are permitted to do, there is naturally more room for them.

The U.S. military of the late twentieth century has not only become more dependent on greater numbers of women, but has also been compelled to rely upon the "outside" skills that an increasing number of women possess. One reason for this is that there are fewer combat roles. Another reason is that jobs in the military are becoming increasingly technological, and civilian skills are therefore more readily transferable to military needs, and vice versa. Because many women have acquired skills in the civilian sector that the military needs—or have indicated an interest in and/or aptitude to learn critical skills deemed "acceptable" for women—they have been increasingly utilized by the armed forces when *man*power skills have been in short supply. Thus, women have become a more visible resource for the military in "other-than-combat" roles.

In this context it is interesting to speculate about the combat infantryman role and its virtual nontransferability, in the legitimate sense, to civilian life. (Even the Army openly admits this non-transferability, listing no counterpart civilian job for military occupational specialty "11B," combat infantryman. The skills of a Navy seaman, on the other hand, are more transferable.) If women, for example, dominated a civilian occupation called "combat infantryman," the Army would be literally forced to use women in such a role. There is, however, little opportunity for women to develop combat skills in a comparable civilian job category, and the combat role is proscribed to military women. The result is a military Catch 22 [no-win situation]: Women do not have an opportunity to learn and therefore cannot be utilized in such a role; women cannot be thus utilized and therefore cannot learn the necessary skills. Some opening in the argument does exist, however, since weapons familiarization and marksmanship skills (two aspects of the combat infantryman role) can be acquired by women through legitimate avenues—for instance, in sporting clubs and in police training. Moreover, some weapons familiarization is provided by the armed forces to its basic trainees, both male and female. The snag in this argument is that men go on to utilize and perfect these skills in the military while women cannot (they are not permitted to do so). Related to this is a third point, concerning "fighting" itself.

The Nature of Combat Is Changing

During the American Revolution and the Civil War, battle lines were hard to draw and define. Women joined men in battle when fighting occurred in their midst. In the modern era, the World War I concept of trench warfare came into being: warfare with clear-cut battle lines and a definite forward edge of the battle area, flanks, and rear area. In such a situation, it was easier to designate areas of fighting and of nonfighting. The advent of long-range weaponry, however, has now made areas other than front lines vulnerable.

Combat has changed in another way. In earlier conflicts, hand-to-hand fighting was often the rule. Today, again through technological development, opposing forces are often discharged from many yards or even many miles away. Indeed, if the opposing force is in an aircraft, a tank, or ship, what is discharged is the vessel itself—face-to-face combat may never even occur. Combat has become increasingly technological and decreasingly personal. In considering the case for women, however, we must examine the issue of combat with the related concepts of gender roles, of spheres of defense, and of citizenship.

Gender Roles and "Spheres of Defense" Are Changing

In the early history of the United States, and on the American frontier, gender roles were more diffuse than they are now. In preindustrial eighteenth-century America [according to scholar Linda Grant DePauw] "in every occupation open to men there also were women working. . . . There was no occupation in which men were engaged that did not include women acting either as practitioners or [as] owners of the business." (Recall that "businesses" were *family* businesses—in the truest sense of the word—at this time.) With industrialization came the separation of work from the home. Men and low-status women moved into the cities to take on new jobs. This was the time when "the cult of true womanhood" was born, a philosophy that assigned to a (high-status) woman a special place, that is, in the home and *outside* the economic order. It was deemed that, owing to characteristics attributed to her gender, economic pursuits were unsuitable for her and she must be protected (by men) from such activities. This was the beginning of the "separate-sphere" philosophy in which each sex had power in a certain area—women in the home, men in the labor force.

Thus, going into the twentieth century, many women were unemployed or underemployed and constituted a potential *reserve* of labor power, to be drawn on when labor was in short supply. This happened, of course, during the two world wars, when many men left their jobs to enter the armed forces and these jobs were taken over by women. At this time also, industrialization and standardization made it possible to mass-produce the food, clothing, weapons, and equipment necessary to support enormous armies in the field for prolonged periods. But this required a national effort. Thus it was a "man's job" to fight in the military and a "woman's job" to work in support and service positions so that men could be "freed" from such jobs to do the "main" job. Thus, it was supposed, women and men "fought" in different ways, dictated by their capacities and natures.

As women have come to participate more extensively in the educational and economic institutions of the United States, gender roles have begun to change and the cult of true womanhood has waned. Much concern has been expressed over the appropriate roles for modern women. Perhaps no issue in this area has been more debated than that of women as warriors and, by implication, the role of women in the military in general. Because it is so tied to the topic of women and conscription, we must examine this issue of women in combat roles before we can get a complete answer to the question of why women have historically been excluded from compulsory military service.

The Continental Army of the American Revolution needed every fighting person it could get. The war was waged on home soil and women fought alongside men. Moreover, the nation's economic base was an agricultural one in which gender roles were somewhat more diffuse than was later the case during industrialization. Thus, because it was a crisis (an emergency during which usual norms might be temporarily suspended), because it was a domestic conflict, and because gender roles were more overlapping, women could contribute to the war effort in both traditional and nontraditional (nontypical) ways. Women were "allowed" to fight. This "right to fight" was later taken away from them by the first-class citizens (men) who made the rules governing military service when the crisis was over. Congress did occasionally recognize the bravery of these female veterans and reward them with pensions, but it did not want them to continue their combat roles once the war was over. Of course, the easiest way to stop them was to prevent them from serving in the armed forces at all, since most of the jobs in the Army and Navy involved combat roles. Men wanted these jobs for themselves. Other supportive jobs, like logistical support and medical care, were just as necessary and probably no less difficult, but they were less glorified jobs and could be done by nonpersons, such as women volunteers, servants, blacks, and other minorities.

Why were these jobs desired by men? One argument is that the opposite of the cult of true womanhood, the cult of true *manhood*, exalted physical aggression and victory as a badge or mark of a man. Combat was seen as a test of virility. It was also a more generalized test of a person's ability to withstand a stress-filled environment for a prolonged period. This type of environment afforded an opportunity for a man to display traits of bravery and leadership (again considered to be marks of manhood), for which he could be recognized and glorified. Men knew that a combat environment might also prompt individual reactions and emotions of a sexually exciting nature, which, according to the cult of true womanhood, women should not experience. Thus, military service, but in particular, combat experience, was (and still is) conceptualized as a rite of passage to "manliness" and therefore to "manhood." It was unnecessary, then, to have women in combat because "manhood" by definition was something that women could never achieve, just as men, by definition, could never achieve "womanhood." The armed forces were thus deemed an exclusively (or predominately) male club to which women were denied admission, or, if admitted, a club in which they could not gain access to the highest ranks and "inner circle" because of this combat exclusion. As DePauw notes:

> This policy, which most people assume protects women, actually keeps them from entering a number of prestigious specialties that are considerably less dangerous and less demanding physically than some of the noncombat jobs women are presently eligible for. Although the overwhelming majority of today's generals are not in combat assignments, experience in such assignments is essential to get to the upper ranks at the Pentagon.

Yet the matter is today, even more than in the past, defini-
tional. Women have "engaged or been engaged by an enemy in
armed conflict," have been "in a geographical area designated
as a combat/hostile fire zone by the Secretary of Defense," and
have "received hostile fire pay and combat awards" [according
to the Department of Defense]. Therefore, even though
women have been under the same conditions—and even
fought—in battle as have men, their roles have not been considered to be "combat" *by definition*, thanks largely to the influence of the concept of separate spheres and the cults of
true womanhood and true manhood. This leads us now to examine the final aspect of our question concerning women and
conscription, the concept of the "citizen-soldier."

The Concept of Citizenship Is Changing

An individual's relationship to the State can find expression in
several forms for "the term *citizen* serves to highlight and
symbolize the dramatic transformation of the individual's relationship to the state that occurred with the breakdown of
European feudalism and the rise of nationalistic democracies."
But citizenship, the privilege and status of only a minority of
the population during the early days of the American Republic, has come to be a much more inclusive phenomenon. The
"noncitizen" category historically encompassed such groups as
slaves, servants, women, aliens, and other marginal and excluded populations.

Just as the concept of "citizen" underwent a period of considerable change during the fourteenth through eighteenth
centuries, so did the concept of "soldier"—that is, an armed
combatant of a nation or ruler. Historically, common soldiers
serving in armies of a particular nation or ruler were not necessarily citizens of the State; rather, they were much more
likely to be slaves, conquered peoples, mercenaries, or members of a warrior caste. Military *leaders* on the other hand,
were likely to be citizens and members of a ruling elite. In

particular, armored knights were those who both held an hereditary title and could afford the proper regalia and entourage; likewise, the mounted cavalry who later held the place of honor on the battlefield, had to be members of the nobility.

In the eighteenth century, the time of the American and French revolutions, the two previously distinct historical concepts of "citizen" and "soldier" merged into a new concept, the "citizen-soldier." Citizens, however, were still a minority of the American population. That is, they were free white males—no woman could be a "citizen." Because women were considered to be *outside* the citizen structure (non-persons), they could not vote or take part in the political process or be in decision-making positions in the governmental and military spheres lest they make laws and policies regarding their own roles and participation. Men in these positions made such decisions for them. Thus women could not be "citizen-soldiers" because they could not be "citizens." The rights and obligations of citizens, including the citizen-soldier function, were extended neither to women nor to other non-citizen classes.

In the eighteenth and nineteenth centuries, the citizen-soldier role was finally extended to these groups. What is unique about the case of women, however, is that they were, and still are, offered only non-combat roles—"their 'right to fight' has been constrained." It has been argued that women have not been subject to compulsory military service because they have the right *but not the obligation* to serve in the military. This view merely supports the historical argument that women constitute a "special category" of citizens, those who do not have either the rights or the duties of full citizenship.

The citizenship issue is, then, a clue to why women have not been included in draft legislation. But there is another angle to this. Service in the armed forces has actually been a pathway to citizenship for many groups who were thus "given the opportunity to prove their loyalty through defense of the state" [according to scholars David R. Segal, Noral Scott Kinzer, and John C. Woelfel]. However, women have served in the armed forces both before and after becoming citizens, in the sense of their assumption of certain citizenship rights, such as property ownership, educational access, enfranchisement. But if women have served in the armed forces, have they not then "proven their loyalty through defense of the state"? The argument here is that their loyalty has not been "proven" because they did not defend the State specifically by bearing arms.

Besides the citizenship argument, other explanations can be advanced as to why women have historically been excluded from compulsory military service. One of these concerns spheres of defense. It was not necessary, for example, to draft women to engage in work that would help to support and maintain an army in the field (for example, wartime defense work and production) when women *as civilians* were doing the jobs that needed to be done. Another potential explanation takes changing international relationships into account. In an age when many conflicts are settled over the conference table rather than on the battlefield, the new "fighter" is becoming the ambassador and diplomat, and more and more women are appearing in such negotiating roles. This explanation, however, relates to the citizenship issue: Women are being increasingly—but not totally—recognized in these roles as legitimate representatives of the State.

There is still another important issue related to citizenship. It is argued that in the modern era only the State and, by extension, its legitimate agents have the power to take a life. The combat soldier, the police patrolman, and the judge, for example, are roles in which this power, under certain circumstances, can be exercised. Thus, the issue related to citizenship for women is this: Do women have the institutional right to take a life? If the answer is no, is this, then, one reason such roles are not seen as appropriate for women? Should women have the same rights and authority as men do? Should women, like men, be full citizens? Should women, like men, be legitimate agents of the State? Moreover, there remains the issue of "proving" loyalty: If women were armed ("allowed" to fight), would they use this new freedom in defense of the State or against it?

A Draft Would Be Both Unfair and Unnecessary

Milton Friedman

In 1973 the United States ended the draft it had maintained since 1940. But in 1980, President Jimmy Carter reinstituted the requirement that all young men between ages eighteen and twenty-six had to register with Selective Service, the federal organization that managed the draft. The requirement remains in place. Meanwhile, Carter's requirement reawakened American debates about the merits of not only a military draft but also of national service requirements in general. The following selection, by prominent economist Milton Friedman, is a product of that debate.

In his opposition to both a military draft and national service requirements, Friedman recognizes that an all-volunteer army is hardly perfect. But any national service program would be incredibly cumbersome and expensive, given the size of America's youth population. Furthermore, and in an echo of arguments Daniel Webster made in 1814, it would be a violation of personal freedoms. Friedman is the author of such books as Capitalism and Freedom *as well as dozens of popular and scholarly articles. He won the Nobel Prize for Economics in 1976.*

I want to start by expressing full agreement with Congressman [Pete] McCloskey about our objectives. Unfortunately, we need to have an army, and we need to have a good army and an efficient army. There's no dispute on that, at least between him and me. There may be some other people who will dispute that, but between the two of us there's no dispute about that.

Milton Friedman, "Argument Against National Service," *Registration and the Draft: Proceedings of the Hoover-Rochester Conference on the All-Volunteer Force*, edited by Martin Anderson, Stanford, CA: Hoover Institution Press, 1982. Copyright © 1982 by the Board of Trustees of the Leland Stanford Junior University. All rights reserved under International and Pan-American Copyright Conventions. Reprinted by permission.

The problem is not one of objectives. It is, on the one hand, a problem of methods and on the other hand, a problem of the effect of the methods applied on the rest of our society.

We need an effective military for a democratic and free society. We do *not* need a military that would be effective for a totalitarian society, and that is a very, very important and basic difference. I know that Congressman McCloskey agrees with me on that, too. We disagree on what techniques will achieve the most effective military force for a free and open society.

Unaccustomed as I am on this kind of issue to quoting the *New York Times*, I have in front of me an Op-Ed column that brings out some of these issues in a very effective way. The column is entitled, "Why Not Draft the Next Congress?" and I hope you will pardon me if I read few excerpts from it.

> The All-Volunteer Congress has proved to be a failure. Its cost is extremely high, and there is not a proportional representation of minorities. There are also many doubts about the honesty and intelligence of the recent volunteers. Many of Congress's recent failures are owing to the low quality of its composition. A change is needed. This country can no longer afford the high cost of the volunteer system. Nor can it tolerate the low level of performance and reliability. Conscription appears to be the only way to get a decent Congress at an affordable price. . . . Some people object to the idea of conscription in itself. But rather than being a moral evil, Congressional conscription should be seen as giving an opportunity for service to the middle-aged. The draftees would have the chance to serve their country and be a part of an important process, and would also learn a lot in the process. Can we allow our national interest to be determined by an overpaid, racially unbalanced, and psychologically unstable pack of volunteers? Our national interests can only be served by a balanced selection of people from all parts of society.

I've read only a small part of this piece, but I recommend the whole of it to you as an extremely effective document for bringing out the implications of departing from volunteer service.

The plain fact is that maintaining an armed force of 2 million people in a democratic free society is a tough job. It's bound to be done imperfectly. It's bound to generate difficulties. As was brought out very effectively in Professor [Phillip] Bobbitt's paper, the farther grass always looks greener. Every system that you adopt is going to have some evils. It's going to have some problems.

The All-Volunteer Force, as it is now being implemented, has some real problems. There's no doubt about that. Congressman McCloskey pointed to some of them, though I think on the whole he exaggerates them. It has some real problems, but so, in my opinion, does a draft—far *worse* problems. Universal national service has some real problems that I'll come to, in my opinion *far worse* problems.

The danger is that we tend to run from the evils we know to those we don't know. We see the system we now have, where the problems have emerged and are visible, and are tempted to move to another system, for which the problems are in the future.

This is the *normal* political operating mechanism. Why do we have so many bad laws? Because legislators invariably tend to point to real evils, describe fine objectives, and then enact programs that are not well suited to respond to those evils or achieve those objectives. There's a strong tendency on the political level to operate in terms of what ought to be done, and to brush aside the more fundamental question of how do you do it.

The national service rhetoric, which Congressman McCloskey adopts, has a great deal of appeal. It *seems* very reasonable to say that all young men owe their country service. But I hasten to add that its appeal is always in general terms and not in specific terms. On this I quote from Professor [William R.] King's paper given earlier at this conference, expressing a favorable view toward national service: "I am not certain that any *particular* national service proposal would, in fact, be superior to the All-Volunteer Force or to the draft." I believe that what you will find, if you take all the people who have expressed preferences for national service, is that each one has a different plan in mind. And none of them likes the other fellow's plan. There may be a good deal of support for national service *in general*, but there is very little support for any particular program.

Part of the appeal of the idea of national service is due to an intellectual confusion between two very different systems. One is universal military service, such as exists, for example, in Switzerland and in Israel. If you have a country which needs the service of all young men, and maybe young women, for its defense—essentially all able-bodied citizens—then a reasonably equitable and fair way to impose a tax on the people is simply to require everybody to serve, to see that everybody is trained, to see that all are available to come to the defense of their country.

America Does Not Need Millions of Soldiers

But that is *not* the situation in the United States. As Congressman McCloskey pointed out, we need at most to recruit something like one out of every five young men, or one of every ten men and women. I say "at most" because I believe that a superior policy of manning our armed forces would place less emphasis on obtaining people averaging 18.569 years of age. Together with retaining people over longer periods, such a reform would reduce substantially the number of people that would have to be recruited each year.

Be that as it may, for purposes of argument let us take the numbers that are now cited: at most we have to recruit one out of four or five males, or one out of ten young people. Under those circumstances, universal *military* service is simply not a feasible proposition. It would be necessary to train 2 million young men a year and 1.5 million of those would be irrelevant. Nobody really proposes that we require 2 million men a year to undergo military service in order to be able to get 300,000 or 400,000 men a year.

Universal *national* service is a wholly different thing. Universal national service is not universal military service. It is a system under which every young man or every young man and every young woman, depending on how it is done, is required to put in a year or two of so-called compulsory service in forms designated by somebody-or-other. . . .

If we . . . consider national service in general, I submit to you that it solves no problems that we now have with the All-Volunteer Force and creates vast new problems. If we're talking about a comprehensive universal national service—if it's something more than a back-door approach to a lottery draft—we'd have to handle 4 million people a year, men and women. If we suppose a two-year tour of duty, that means 8 *million* people to administer. Who allocates them to jobs? Who decides what they do? Who determines their training? What power to put in the hands of people who would seek it!

Note also that none of what those people would do would be useful work: it would all be make-work. If you tried to have them do useful work, the trade unions of this country would be down on you like a ton of bricks. It would be work which some people believe *other* people ought to be paying for, because the whole purpose would be to enable a group of administrators to direct young people into activities that young people did not want to engage in. If they wanted to engage in it now, we would already have a system of universal national service. Right now every young man in the country, and every young women in the country, has an opportunity to volunteer for a whole variety of tasks, paid and unpaid, and that is equivalent to a system of universal national service. But, unlike Congressman McCloskey's proposal, it is a truly voluntary system of universal national service, not a compulsory system.

I must say that we don't learn very much from history, and I really cannot do better than to quote Senator Robert Taft, who, in discussing the issue of the draft before World War II, said,

> The principle of a compulsory draft is basically wrong. If we must use compulsion to get an army, why not use compulsion to get men for other essential tasks? Why not draft labor for essential occupations at wages lower than the standard? In short, the logic requires a complete regimentation of most labor, and the assignment of jobs to every man. This is actually done in the communist and fascist state, which we are now apparently seeking to emulate.

In light of that comment it is interesting to consider who has favored and who has opposed the idea of using compulsion to man our military. With respect to the draft in the United States, the situation is quite clear: in the main, conservatives have been opposed to conscription, whereas liberals have supported it. The wartime draft was barely passed. In 1946, Robert Taft, all by himself, prevented President [Harry S.] Truman from using the draft to return striking railroad workers to their jobs. [Conservative Arizona senator] Barry Goldwater in 1964 came out in opposition to the draft. President Richard Nixon and his Secretary of Defense, Melvin Laird, were the main movers in ending the draft in 1973. The one exception is that of [presidential candidate] Adlai Stevenson, who in 1956, under the urging of [liberal economist] John Kenneth Galbraith with respect to the only issue on which he and I agree, came out in opposition to the draft.

In the [recent] congressional debates on the All-Volunteer Force, one of its main opponents was [liberal Massachusetts senator] Teddy Kennedy. If you look at the overall record, you will see that those people who have opposed the voluntary force have generally consisted of two very different types: one group, the strong military types under the influence of some of the professional military, and the other what we now call, in our debased language, liberals.

If you look at the record in the United States, the first extensive treatment of universal national Service was by Edward Bellamy in 1888, in his book *Looking Backward*, which is a socialist Utopian novel. Ever since, universal national service has been supported primarily by modern liberals, by people who believe in a collective society. It has tended to be *opposed* by people like myself who believe in a *free* society, who believe that individuals should separately be free to choose their activities in accordance with their values, and that if some of us want to hire others of them to do certain jobs for us, we have to pay them what it takes to get them to do it for us and not impose it on them by force directly or indirectly.

My general conclusion is that universal national service would be a monstrosity. If adopted, it would undermine the basic foundations of this free society, and it is something that we should avoid like a plague.

I do not believe that Congressman McCloskey, if he really looked seriously at the consequences of what he proposes and what would develop out of his proposals, would like what he found. This is an experience that has happened over and over again. The proponents of plans like this almost invariably turn out to be the people who later are the very ones who least like the Frankenstein they have created. I believe that Congressman McCloskey would find himself one of that group.

CHAPTER 4

The Military Draft
in Recent Times

Chapter Preface

After the Cold War ended in 1991, and with it the perceived need for large standing armies and continual military readiness, many countries that had maintained conscription or national service began to end it. For them issues of personal freedom, the expense of a draft, and changing military technologies which lessened the need for soldiers greatly reduced the desirability of conscription. Of the major European powers, only Germany continues as military training requirements, although even the Germans are considering drawing them down.

The nation of Israel still has comprehensive national service requirements, both for men and for women. Its leaders consider themselves surrounded by potential enemies and therefore think the country needs to always be ready for warfare. Some Israeli draftees, however, in ways reminiscent of American involvement in the Vietnam War, have become "refuseniks." These young people refuse to serve out of opposition to some of their country's policies.

In the United States, debate over the draft was reawakened with the Iraq War that began in 2003. Although most political and military leaders claim that a draft is no longer desirable nor necessary a few, notably Michigan congressman Charles Rangel, argue that military service falls unfairly on America's poor. A draft, properly designed, would prevent that as well as ensure that no American family could keep itself distant from conflicts like that in Iraq as well as the policies that enabled it. Making the issue even more pressing is the fact that continuing conflict in Iraq, as well as on the military more generally, have required what some term a "back-door draft." In this, active-duty service people find their tours extended, reservists and National Guardsmen are required to serve in ways they might be unready for, and even a few who have been discharged from the service have been called back, sometimes after years. Author Philip Gold suspects that such developments might further enflame debates over not only the draft itself but also over whether women or homosexuals might be subject to any new draft.

An Israeli Draftee Seeks Moral Conditions for Service

Itamar Shahar

The nation of Israel has one of the most comprehensive drafts in the modern world. National service is compulsory for almost all men and women of eighteen years or older: Men commonly serve in the national army, known as the Israeli Defense Force (IDF), for three years, while women serve for two years. Indeed, serving in the IDF is a common rite of passage for young Israelis.

Not all young Israelis accept their terms of service, however. In the following selection, Itamar Shahar describes his opposition to continued service in the light of the IDF's treatment of Israel's Palestinian population. After a 1967 war with an Arab coalition, Israel occupied regions known as the West Bank and Gaza Strip, which are mostly inhabited by Arab Palestinians. As the resulting tensions continued, and even mounted, into the twenty-first century, Shahar found himself unable to continue his IDF service. He cites not only his view of Israel's treatment of the Palestinians but also his concern over what the occupation has done to Israel itself. In this he joins a long line of so-called refuseniks, many of whom have been sent to jail for their refusal to serve.

I the undersigned, Itamar Shahar (Military ID 7015540), hereby declare that I am no longer willing to continue to serve in the IDF [Israeli Defense Force]. The actions the army has been conducting these past two years in the West Bank and Gaza Strip are immoral and non-legitimate, injuring and killing hundreds of innocent civilians; denying medical attention, education and a livelihood to millions of human beings;

actions of deportation, demolishing homes and uprooting fruit groves—these are deeds which cannot be tolerated, certainly one cannot take part therein or in the body perpetrating them. The Israeli government's policy of occupation, repression and colonisation is the cause of the bloodshed in our region, whose principal casualties are civilians on both sides. Accordingly, if we wish to live a dignified, free and peaceful existence here, we must fight the occupation that brings calamity upon both peoples, and refuse to carry out any action that serves to perpetuate the occupation.

In my view, the state of Israel, like any other state, has the right to maintain a popular armed force to be deployed in defence of the lives of the state's citizens, when there are no alternatives available. Possessing the ability and the willingness to contribute to this army, I enlisted in August 2000 for combat service in the IDF. Two months after my induction, at the end of September 2000, violence erupted in the Gaza Strip and West Bank. Since then, I have served many months in the bloc of Jewish settlements in the Gaza Strip known as the "Katif Bloc".

In the course of those months, I made a close acquaintance with the daily reality of occupation: the humiliating delays and searches at road blocks; the deplorable exploitation of Palestinian workers by the Jewish settlers who took their land; the settlers who are willing to neglect the physical and psychological wellbeing of their children for material gain or out of fundamentalist religious conviction; the callousness of the military authorities towards the needs of the Palestinian population thrown upon their mercies; and the psychological change undergone by 18-year-old youngsters suddenly granted the power to dominate other human beings. It is precisely this close acquaintance that has led me to conclude that it is out of the question to behave in a moral manner in circumstances founded upon the relationship between occupier and occupied. Initially, I thought it might be possible to try and improve these circumstance to a degree, but ultimately I understood that the only way for an ordinary soldier to defend the wellbeing of all concerned, Palestinians and Israelis, is by refusing to take a hand in the occupation apparatus.

After talking the matter over with my superiors, and after a number of months during which I was not assigned any duties, I was posted to serve as instructor of the intelligence section at a basic training camp in the Negev. Naively, I believed that this duty would be confined to contributing to the defence of the citizens of Israel, and I was overjoyed at being given duties that would perhaps enable me to influence the outlook of young soldiers commencing their military service. But I soon learned that even this task constitutes direct assistance to the occupation apparatus.

War Crimes

In April 2002, before being posted to my new assignment, the Israeli army commenced—on instructions from the government—a series of barbaric attacks on Palestinian population centres in the West Bank, entailing violation of all the most basic moral norms as expressed not merely in international conventions, but also in the laws of the state of Israel and the ethical code of the IDF itself. Even in war, there are rules that may not be violated. In April 2002, the gravest of war crimes were committed, not only by ordinary soldiers in the field, but also by senior officers and the political echelons, the latter handing down to the combat units orders that were flagrantly illegal. These events further exacerbated the doubts and perplexities bearing upon me: how could I be in the ranks of a body, a considerable portion of whose present actions constitute terrorism against innocent civilians?

The name of the operation—"Defensive Wall"—was a cover for the systematic demolition of the physical and human infrastructure of Palestinian civilian society, simultaneously destroying any hope of reconciliation between the two peoples in the foreseeable future. Now that on the Palestinian side of the green line nothing is left but physical destruction and human beings who are demoralised, hungry and oppressed, [Israeli prime minister Ariel] Sharon can easily prove his claims that the other side is "no partner for peace".

My act of refusal is not entirely altruistic: I am not refusing merely over the violation of the human rights of the people of the West Bank and Gaza—even though in my view those are perfectly adequate grounds—but also for the benefit of Israeli society, in which I live. The destinies of the two peoples are interconnected, and the harm inflicted upon the Palestinians prompts some of them to adopt non-legitimate measures of harming innocent citizens of Israel, so that fear has become a central component of our routine existence. Thirty-five years of occupation have made Israeli society violent and racist, a society wherein many live in poverty and ignorance. As though that were not sufficient, we are destroying the last lingering chance of achieving peace in this region. If we do not sober up, as members of the dominant nation, to allow the Palestinian people to achieve its legitimate rights, we shall find ourselves in an even worse plight than that which we have reached.

In my view, a decent moral person will consent to serve in the national army on two basic conditions:

1. The army shall serve exclusively to defend the lives and liberty of the state's citizens, and no other purpose.

2. The state and its security agencies shall, in all their actions, observe a basic moral code arising out of the equal value of all human beings, as expressed in international conventions such as the Geneva Convention for the Protection of Civilians in Wartime and the Universal Declaration of Human Rights.

In view of the gross violation of these conditions by the Israeli government and its army, and in view of the fact that any assignment with the IDF entails assistance to immoral and non-legitimate policies which bring disaster upon the entire region, I hereby declare that, as of this week, I no longer regard myself as an IDF soldier obliged to comply with military orders. The moment the aforementioned conditions are fulfilled adequately, I shall be willing to place myself at the disposal of any service required for the citizens of the state in which I live.

European Countries Now Reject the Draft and the United States Should Too

Cindy Williams

During the Cold War, which lasted from 1945 to 1991 and pit-
ted in a tense standoff the democratic West against the commu-
nist Soviet Union and its allies, most nations involved main-
tained a draft. It was considered a necessary safeguard in the
event of a large-scale ground conflict similar to World War II.
After the Cold War ended in 1991, the Soviet Union split up into
numerous independent (and often democratic) states, while
Eastern European countries, former Soviet allies, also turned to
democracy and, in some cases, subdivided themselves. A number
of these new states have joined, or hope to join, the NATO alli-
ance, or North Atlantic Treaty Organization. They have often
found that a draft is no longer desirable or necessary. They have
followed such older powers as France and Spain in ending or
downsizing the draft.

In the following selection, scholar Cindy Williams argues that
the United States should follow their model and reject any plans
to revive a draft. Voluntary armies, she claims, are more appro-
priate twenty-first-century conflicts and avoid the social conflict
that comes along with a draft. Williams is a scholar in the Secu-
rity Studies Program at the Massachusetts Institute of Technol-
ogy and is the editor of Filling the Ranks: Transforming the
U.S. Military Personnel System.

Although President [George W.] Bush said during
Thursday's [2004 presidential election] debate that he
would keep the all-volunteer system for bringing people into
the military, the Internet continues to buzz with rumors of an

Cindy Williams, "Draft Lessons From Europe," *Washington Post*, October 5, 2004. Copyright © 2004 The Washington Post Company. Reproduced by permission of the author.

imminent reinstatement of the draft. It is a subject thought to be worthy of serious discussion.

This must come as something of a surprise to our NATO [North Atlantic Treaty Organization] allies, who have, over much of the past decade, gotten used to hearing U.S. leaders deride conscription as a relic of the Cold War and describe Europe's military draftees as undertrained, underequipped and undeployable.

Nicholas Burns, the U.S. ambassador to NATO, advised our European partners to get rid of their conscripts. Defense Department officials praised France and Italy for shifting to all-volunteer forces and applauded Germany's decision to trim its number of conscripts. Military leaders encouraged aspiring NATO members to put an end to compulsory service.

The United States halted conscription as the Vietnam War was winding down in 1973, largely in response to political concerns over social and racial inequities. Among NATO's members, Canada, Britain and Luxembourg also have a decades-long tradition of all-volunteer service. But all of NATO's other states—including the new members from the former [communist] East Bloc—relied on conscription to fill their ranks throughout the Cold War.

Since the mid-1990s, though, Belgium, France, Hungary, the Netherlands, Portugal and Spain have ended the draft. The Czech Republic, Italy, Latvia, Romania, the Slovak Republic and Slovenia plan to phase it out within the next several years.

Reasons to End the Draft

Each country ended conscription for its own reasons. Geopolitical factors played some role. After the fall of the Soviet Union, the large conscript armies that underwrote territorial defense during the Cold War seemed an anachronism. For the new members, the protection afforded by NATO reduced the need for large numbers of conscripts.

New military missions also figured in. Conscripts in Europe are often prohibited by law from serving outside their countries, so they are generally unsuitable for NATO's new expeditionary missions. Some countries also found that peacekeeping and the fight against terrorism required longer periods of training than their short terms of conscription allowed.

In addition, ambitions for military transformation—fundamental changes in the way militaries fight, supported by modern information systems and other high-technology equipment—fed into the allies' decisions. Volunteers typically serve longer than draftees. As a result, they often perform better in military tasks requiring a high level of skill. Longer service also translates into lower turnover, which in turn reduces the number of recruits who must be trained each year and cuts costs. Decision makers in some countries hoped to divert savings to new equipment, thus narrowing the gap in modern military capabilities between the United States and the rest of NATO.

But while strategic and military factors clearly mattered, one of the most important reasons for European leaders was a weakening of the legitimacy of the draft. Across much of Europe, conscription was nearly universal during the Cold War, and military service was widely regarded as a duty of citizenship. As countries downsized their militaries, however, the number of draftees required to fill the ranks fell sharply. Eventually, so few eligible youth were called up that the draft began to seem unfair. Once that happened, young people quickly lost confidence in conscription as an institution of national life. By the time Spain ended compulsory service, some 75 percent of draft-eligible young men claimed conscientious-objector status. In the former Communist countries, outright draft avoidance and the costs of enforcement became serious problems. In nation after nation—as in the United States during the Vietnam War—popular support for conscription plummeted, dragging public support for the military down with it.

The United States Should Follow Its Own Advice

If the United States really is contemplating a return to the draft, it should give some thought to its own advice to European militaries. While not suited to every circumstance, volunteer forces are indeed more efficient and better suited to the expeditionary missions we expect and the high-technology capabilities we want for our military.

Even more important, the charges of unfairness across Europe echo a lesson we should have learned in the 1960s: A draft that is substantially less than universal is not politically sustainable in a modern liberal democracy. Even if the United States had to double the size of the deployable Army, our military would still need to draw in only a small fraction of American youth each year. And a draft that leaves most people out will inevitably appear unfair to those who are forced in.

America's future decisions about its own all-volunteer force will be national ones; what our allies do or say about it will not play a part. Nevertheless, the United States could learn a great deal from the nations that—for reasons of their own—followed our advice and dropped the draft.

America Needs an Open, Honest Discussion of the Draft

Philip Gold

The context of the following selection was the continued American military involvement in Iraq in 2004 and the concerns that the military commitment there was overextending our troops as well as falling unfairly on certain social groups. The author, columnist Philip Gold, suspects that these concerns might lead to serious consideration of a new military draft. He hopes, however, that any new draft avoids the unfairness and other problems of earlier drafts, most notably that of the Vietnam War era. He also hopes that any draft is considered in the light of such issues as the roles of women and homosexuals as well as the concern, common in any discussion of the draft, of whether governments have the right to limit people's freedoms in this manner.

Gold served in the U.S. Marines for eleven years. He has a PhD in history from Georgetown University, where he taught for fourteen years, and is the author of six books and over eight hundred articles.

There is a process in American politics by which the unthinkable becomes the inevitable. Proposals are floated. Warnings are issued. Intentions are officially denied. But the proposals don't go away. Soon enough, they become fixtures of national debate. And soon enough, the official denials don't seem quite so strenuous. Gradually, the burden of proof shifts from those who want to do something to those who oppose it. Then that something happens . . . and we wonder how it ever came to this.

For well over a year now, proponents of renewed conscription have been offering up their ideas. Some on the left favor

Philip Gold, "The Draft: Unthinkable? Think Again," *Washington Law and Politics*, April–May 2004. Reproduced by permission of the author.

"national service with military and nonmilitary options" as a way of spreading the burdens, teaching kids patriotism and sacrifice and getting all kinds of allegedly desirable work done via the creation of a monstrous new teenager-herding bureaucracy. In January 2003, Democratic Congressman Charles Rangel introduced legislation to this effect. He was backed by the usual-suspect academics, especially sociologist Charles Moskos, who has been pushing national service for decades.

Meanwhile, the neocon right [an influential group of so-called "neoconservatives" who favor activist U.S. military intervention around the world] and a few "outspoken" generals rest their argument on military necessity: the necessity generated by our own chosen actions and commitments. Policing the world takes people. Iraq is wearing out our Army. The reserves and National Guard, already strained by systematic overuse during the Clinton years [administration of President Bill Clinton from 1993 to 2001] and domestic duties since 9/11, approach collapse. Predictably, the [President George W.] Bush administration has denied any intention of reinstating conscription—even as it increases staffing on the local boards of the Selective Service System and keeps people from leaving the active and reserve forces by a legal gimmick called "stop-loss orders." Once those orders expire, a mass exodus may occur.

Indeed, it may already have begun. The damage is long-term and, no matter who wins [the presidential election] in November [2004] this is not an issue that is going to go away.

Public Debate Is Needed

I oppose conscription, save *in extremis* [in extreme circumstances]. Most Americans do. But we should welcome a public debate as a means of clarifying a few matters past, present and future.

The Vietnam-era draft was monstrous, but not because it fell disproportionately on the poor and minorities. Vietnam was, broadly speaking, a middle-class war; so were the casualties. And of the 36.8 million men who turned draft-age between 1965 and 1973, nearly half wore a uniform in some capacity or other. The draft had two deeper problems, which still resonate today.

First, there was then, as there is today, a vast excess of bodies over and above the military requirements. So the pre-Vietnam draft became an exercise in social engineering—or, as it was called back then, "channeling." A complex and generous latticework of deferments and exemptions encouraged young men to beat the draft by engaging in socially desirable activities such as going to college, grad school, more grad school or getting married, making babies, making more babies, etc.

This was essentially the draft we used to fight Vietnam: a draft designed to keep people out. The lottery system that replaced it from 1970 to 1973 [and ended many exceptions and deferments] represented an improvement. But that lottery was a buy-off until the draft could be ended entire. Today a lottery system would face the same problem: a major excess of bodies beyond requirements. The same basic inequity—some serve, many don't—would pertain, unless we hauled off a couple million teenagers a year for the sake of "fairness." And let's be honest about what "military and nonmilitary options" really means.

The second monstrous feature of the Vietnam-era draft entailed the belief that draftees could be sent anywhere to do anything. Throughout the Cold War, most Western democracies drafted. But conscription was tied, legally and customarily, to homeland defense or limited NATO [North Atlantic Treaty Organisation] service. Only America strewed the planet with its draftees—a mistake we're making again, now that our reservists and guard members serve as the equivalent of conscripts.

Would renewed conscription be "homeland defense only," or would it simply provide future presidents with large quantities of semiskilled, expendable labor?

And what of women? When [President] Jimmy Carter reinstituted draft registration in 1980, the Supreme Court ruled (*Rostker v. Goldberg*) that women didn't have to register. They based their decision on traditional deference to the military's unique nature and requirements. But that was nearly a quarter century ago. Women now constitute 15 percent of our forces; the percentage is rising. They serve aboard warships and as pilots and flight crews; they routinely face danger and combat in Iraq. Can conscription of women any longer be opposed on the basis of military necessity? The opposite would seem more likely.

And would the gay exclusion—a policy originally grounded in bureaucratic convenience, not military reality—still hold, even in its present "Don't ask/don't tell" faux [false] compromise?

A Debate Would Tell Us a Lot

No, the draft isn't likely anytime soon. But a debate over conscription would tell us a lot about the kind of people we've become. It would be a glimpse of ourselves, asking and maybe answering such questions as:

Do we take our "global leadership" so seriously that we're willing to grant our government unlimited access to our young people?

Are we still prepared to deny half our population one of the most fundamental rights and responsibilities of citizenship: full participation in the common defense?

Are we still prepared to exclude an entire class of citizens—gay people—from service on the basis of what some of them might do . . . and of how others might react to them?

And, perhaps most important, what would a new draft debate tell us about our ability to speak to each other as citizens, in meaningful words? Could we even do it anymore? Or have we grown so used to being spun, manipulated, talked down to and twisted, so used to hissy-fitting and diatribes that we couldn't muster the vocabulary for a serious discussion, even if we wanted to? The vocabulary, or the civility?

The War in Iraq Demands Shared Sacrifice

Charles Rangel

In the following selection Michigan congressman Charles Rangel reiterates his call for a new, universal draft in the United States. He first introduced a bill that would require such a draft in January 2003, during the months when the United States was both preparing and defending its planned invasion of Iraq (which took place in March 2003).

In both instances Rangel, a Democrat, was interested not so much in a larger military but in a fairer one. He notes that American forces are made up mostly of those seeking economic opportunity as well as a chance to serve. Those from more comfortable backgrounds rarely join up in large numbers. Rangel implies that if almost everyone were required to serve, rich as well as poor, there would be less inclination to support military adventures that many see as questionable.

Rangel's 2007 proposal came after President George W. Bush proposed expanding the number of troops in Iraq. Rangel notes that the military commitment there has already resulted in an overextension of the U.S. military, and that many troops face repeated tours of duty, call-backs, and other forms of a "backdoor" draft.

I have reintroduced my bill [in January 2007] to reinstate the draft [after a first introduction in January 2003] not because I support the war in Iraq or the President's [George W. Bush] plan to escalate the conflict. The reason is my belief that if Americans are to be placed in harm's way, all of us, from every income group and position in society, must share the burden of war.

Charles Rangel, "Congressman Rangel Introduces New Bill to Reinstate the Military Draft," news release, January 11, 2007.

That has not been the case so far. The overwhelming majority of our troops fighting in Iraq are young men and women who have chosen to enlist because military service is an economic opportunity. They are motivated by enlistment bonuses up to $40,000 and additional thousands in scholarships to attend college. They are from urban and rural communities where there is high unemployment and few opportunities to pursue the American Dream. My colleague, Congressman Ike Skelton [of Missouri], has confirmed that fact while pointing out the patriotism of these young men and women, and I agree with him.

It is time that all Americans—including the wealthy—be given the opportunity to prove their patriotism as well, by saluting when the flag goes up and defending their country in wartime. A military draft would ensure that.

My bill requires that, during wartime, all legal residents of the U.S. between the ages of 18 and 42 would be subject to a military draft, with the number determined by the President. No deferments would be allowed beyond the completion of high school, up to age 20, except for conscientious objectors or those with health problems. A permanent provision of the bill mandates that those not needed by the military be required to perform two years of civilian service in our sea and airports, schools, hospitals, and other facilities.

I don't see how anyone who supports the War in Iraq would not support reinstatement of the draft.

The President announced last night [January 2007] his intention to send an additional 21,000 U.S. troops to Iraq. The military is at the breaking point with more than 50 percent of our combat troops already deployed in Iraq. The question is: where will the additional troops—including those that may follow if the war is escalated further—come from?

An Overextended Military

The 21,000 soldiers that the President was talking about will not be fresh troops. Many of them are already on the ground in Iraq and will have their deployments extended. Almost 250,000 of the troops currently deployed in Iraq have served more than one tour, and some have been deployed as many as six times.

Since the start of the war, more than 14,000 discharged army veterans—members of the Individual Ready Reserve [the reserve made up of some of those long out of the service]—have been called back from their jobs and families to serve in Iraq. Thousands have had their tours extended under so-called stop-loss orders [which extend duty beyond one's agreed term].

The forced, repeated deployments of nominally volunteer troops not only violates the spirit of the contract with these soldiers, it is a cruel and unfair erosion of the principle of shared sacrifice which has been totally absent in the prosecution of this war.

Last night President Bush warned the nation that we are in for further sacrifices in Iraq. But the truth is, the sacrifice is being borne exclusively by the 1 million-plus troops who have served, and their families. Three thousand have made the ultimate sacrifice and 22,000 have been wounded and maimed.

The rest of us have not been called upon to make any sacrifice at all. It is the first time in an American war in which the populace has not even been asked to bear the burden of the war's cost. Fighting this war with borrowed money, we are leaving our children and their children to pick up the check that as of now is roughly $500 billion, and counting.

A Draft Is a Misuse of Resources and Creates an Army of Misfits

Walter E. Williams

The following article by economist Walter E. Williams, published in the conservative online magazine Townhall.com, *is a response to Democratic congressman Charles Rangel's proposal to introduce mandatory national service for all young Americans, including military service where appropriate. Rangel first proposed the notion in January 2003 and then reiterated it in late 2006 and early 2007.*

Williams, in contrast to Rangel, strongly favors an all-volunteer army. He suspects that a larger military would be accompanied by a greater desire to use that military, as opposed to Rangel's contention that a universal draft might inspire more careful thinking along those lines. Williams also claims that a drafted army would be unreasonably expensive, not least since it removes the labor (and other economic activities, such as purchases) from the civilian economy. He cites his personal experiences, noting in addition that drafting him did not necessarily result in the appearance of an obedient, reliable soldier.

Williams is the John M. Olin Distinguished Professor of Economics at George Mason University.

Congressman Charles Rangel plans to introduce legislation calling for reinstatement of the military draft. He says, "There's no question in my mind that this president and this administration would never have invaded Iraq, especially on the flimsy evidence that was presented to the Congress, if indeed we had a draft and members of Congress and the administration thought that their kids from their communities would be placed in harm's way."

Walter E. Williams, "Reinstating the Military Draft," *Townhall.com*, December 27, 2006. Reproduced by permission of Walter E. Williams and Creators Syndicate, Inc.

Rep. Rangel, D-N.Y., has it completely backward in terms of incentives created by the draft. Let's apply a bit of economic logic to it, but first get a pet peeve of mine out of the way: The term "draft" is a euphemism for what is actually "confiscation of labor services." The Defense Department can get all the military personnel it wants on an all-volunteer basis; it could simply raise wages. Indeed, there exists a wage whereby even I would volunteer my services.

The draft is needed when the military wants to pay soldiers wages lower than those earned in the non-military sector of our economy. When we did have a draft, as in 1950s, look at who was and was not drafted. The commander in chief at that time, President Dwight Eisenhower, wasn't drafted. Neither were members of the Joint Chiefs of Staff. Generals and other high-ranking officers weren't drafted. Who was drafted? Recruits, and it's not hard to understand why. A newly inducted recruit's pay was $68 a month. The pay of the commander in chief, Joint Chiefs of Staff, generals and other officers were many multiples higher than a recruit's pay. It's not difficult to understand why drafting recruits was necessary. Some argue that depending on an all-volunteer military is too expensive. That's wrong. The true cost of having a man in the military is what society has to forgo, what economists call opportunity costs. Say a man worked producing televisions for which he was paid $1,000 a month. If he's drafted, he's not producing $1,000 worth of televisions. The sacrificed $1,000 worth of televisions is part of the cost of his being in the military whether he's paid $68 a month or nothing a month. One effect of the draft is to understate the full cost of military operations.

A Drop in Pay and a Waste of Resources

In 1959, prior to my being drafted, I drove a taxi for Yellow Cab Company in Philadelphia earning about $400 a month. In August that year, I started earning $68 a month. The military budget saw a cost of $68 as opposed to the $400 worth of taxi services society had to forgo. Simple economics suggests that if the cost of a resource is understated, there will be bias toward greater and more wasteful use of that resource. Contrary to Rep. Rangel's assertion, a draft would tend to give rise to greater, not less, use of the military. Today's all-volunteer military consists of high-quality soldiers and fewer misfits than yesteryear. I speak from experience; I was one of those misfits. Being drafted meant lower wages and a waste of my time. To make matters worse, my basic training was at Fort Jackson, S.C., and afterward, I was stationed at Fort Stewart, Ga. This was 1959, and I didn't have a very good orientation on Southern customs and its standards for blacks. There were many self-created adjustment problems associated with my activities, such as: organizing black soldiers to go to the post dance on the "wrong" night; sloppy soldiering; being court-martialed and winning; investigations of me, at least being tailed, by the military authorities; and at-home FBI inquiries of neighbors about Mrs. Williams. The military draft is an offense to the values of liberty, causes misallocation of resources, and there's a higher risk of getting a bunch of misfits. The all-volunteer military does none of this.

Chronology

1793

Revolutionary France introduces the *levée en masse*, the first draft law of modern times. It is designed to recruit three hundred thousand soldiers to help protect France against a threatened invasion from the Austrian Empire. Leaders justify the levy on the grounds that all national citizens must contribute to the common defense.

1798

France enacts a broader conscription law. By 1812 it had drafted over 2,600,000 men into the army.

1812

The U.S. Congress introduces its first draft legislation during the ongoing War of 1812. It is rejected in 1814.

1813

The German state of Prussia, which was later to lead the process of German unification, introduces universal conscription in emulation of France's *levée en masse*. It maintained the draft throughout the nineteenth and into the twentieth centuries. This made Prussia, and after 1871 unified Germany, Europe's most militarized state.

1862

During the American Civil War, the Confederacy passes its first draft law. It makes all white men between the ages of seventeen and thirty five eligible for conscription, although it is possible to gain exemptions or find substitutes. Later Confederate draft laws end the exemptions and substitutions and extend the age range from seventeen to fifty.

1863

The Union passes its first national conscription law, known as the Enrollment Act. It requires men ages eighteen to thirty five to be draft eligible if they are approved by local enrollment boards. Those drafted can choose, however, to find substitutes or pay a "bounty" of three hundred dollars, and many did. Draftees formed only a small percentage of the Union's armies.

1863

Major antidraft riots take place in New York City. Many of the participants are poor Irish immigrants unable to pay the three hundred dollar bounty and who claim that the draft is unfair because it exempts the rich. Further rioting takes place in Boston and other cities.

1915

The first U.S. Citizens Military Camp is established in Plattsburg, New York; other camps follow around the country. Their purpose is to train junior officers for future service in the regular military. Leaders of the Plattsburg movement included General John Macauley Palmer and, from 1916, Grenville Clark. Both advocated universal military training as a form of national service. The Plattsburg movement wound down as the United States entered World War I, but it had a large influence on future discussions of the draft.

1917

After much debate, the United States passes a Selective Service law following American entrance into World War I. It requires all men ages twenty one to thirty one to register (later eighteen to forty five), although ministers, students of the ministry, and a few others were exempt. The law recognized conscientious objection, but generally required noncombat service from those so designated.

1917

The U.S. Supreme Court holds that the federal government has the right to institute a draft. The decision was reached after the World War I conscription law was challenged as unconstitutional.

1918

The United States ends the draft, although strong interests believed that the country should maintain Universal Military Training (UMT) even in peacetime.

1918

The Soviet Union introduces a compulsory draft for men ages eighteen to forty. It faces a period of civil war following the 1917 Russian Revolution, which brings a communist regime to power.

1919

Great Britain and Germany end compulsory conscription.

1926

The United States forms a Joint Army-Navy Selective Service Committee. Its responsibilities include determining manpower needs for future wars and considering new draft proposals.

1930

The Soviet Union expands its draft to include women.

1935

Nazi Germany reinstitutes compulsory military service. From 1939, girls under twenty-five are also required to serve, generally in labor battalions.

1940

With World War II underway, Great Britain adopts an Emergency Powers Defense Bill. It provides for the drafting of men into the armed services and young, unmarried women into industrial and other work.

1940

In July, the United States passes the Burke-Wadsworth bill, its first ever peacetime draft. Highly influenced by the earlier Plattsburg movement, the bill requires all men ages twenty-one to thirty-five to register with Selective Service, with the potential to be drafted for one year of service. The bill takes effect in November.

1941

On December 7, the U.S. naval base at Pearl Harbor in Hawaii is bombed by Japanese forces, bringing the United States into World War II. The 1940 draft bill is broadened to eventually include men ages eighteen to thirty-eight. Those drafted served for the duration of the war plus six months. Eventually, some thirty-six million men register and ten million are drafted. Unlike the earlier legislation, the new draft allows for draftees to be sent anywhere in the world.

1947

The American draft stops when the World War II conscription legislation is not renewed by Congress.

1948

In the face of renewed threats from the Soviet Union and the expansion of the Cold War, the United States reinstitutes the draft. Young men continue to be required to register for Selective Service, although not all are drafted. The draft is renewed in 1950, 1955, 1959, 1963, and 1967.

1948

Great Britain begins to require National Service.

1948

The new state of Israel begins a draft which requires three years of service from young men and two years from young women. Among those exempted are Israeli Arabs.

1952

An attempt to broaden American conscription by introducing mandatory universal military training is defeated in the House of Representatives.

1952

The U.S. Reserve Forces Act is enacted by Congress. It requires those drafted (as well as voluntary enlistees) to be available as military reserves after their terms of active duty service end. The total period of time required, including both active and reserve status, is eight years.

1960

Great Britain ends National Service. The last "National Serviceman" leaves duty in 1963.

1964

Republican presidential candidate Barry Goldwater speaks out against the continued draft on the grounds that it is a violation of personal freedom.

1965

The United States sends its first ground troops to the Vietnam War. Opposition to the war inspires antidraft protests as well as attempts by the government to reform the draft.

1965

The U.S. Supreme Court broadens the definition of conscientious objection to include nontraditional religious or cultural beliefs.

1966

President Lyndon B. Johnson appoints a National Advisory Commission on Selective Service to examine ways to improve the draft. Among its recommendations are to make the draft more equitable by ending the deferments available to college students. These recommendations are largely ignored when the Selective Service Act is renewed in 1967.

1967–1971

Antidraft activity becomes widespread. Many protesters burn their draft cards as a symbolic rejection of the draft. Others become "draft-dodgers" seeking to avoid Vietnam service by going to prison, going underground, or even fleeing the country. Meanwhile, conscientious objector status is granted to thousands.

1969

President Richard M. Nixon changes the U.S. draft to a lottery-based system. While it ends student and other deferments, it also inducts few men into the armed services.

1971

The U.S. Congress extends the 1967 renewal of Selective Service.

1973

The Selective Service Act is not renewed, ending the draft in the United States.

1980

President Jimmy Carter reintroduces the requirement that all young men register with Selective Service, although the draft itself is not renewed. Those who do not register will remain ineligible, among other things, for such federal aid as student loans.

2001–2006

Many Western European nations undertake the shift from National Service to all-volunteer armies. Among their arguments are that volunteers tend to be much better versed in the kinds of technology that modern militaries require. Some nations, notably Germany, Switzerland, and the Scandinavian countries of Norway and Sweden, maintain conscription. In all, young men generally receive military training for less than a year but are then eligible for service as reserves. Some perform non-military national service in institutions such as hospitals.

2003

The United States invades Iraq. Congressman Charles Rangel, a Korean War draftee, introduces a new and broad-ranging draft bill arguing that compulsory military service will make people look at overseas military adventures closely and realistically. Few other politicians support it.

2003–2007

In the face of continued military commitments in Iraq, Afghanistan, and elsewhere in the world, America's volunteer service people face long and repeated tours of duty. Some are subject to a so-called backdoor draft which extends their periods of enlistment beyond original agreements or, in some cases, calls back service people who have been in civilian life for years. Congressman Rangel renews his call for a new draft, but neither other politicians nor military leaders support him.

Organizations to Contact

The editors compiled the following list of organizations concerned with the topics discussed in this book. The descriptions are from materials provided by the organizations. All have information available for interested readers. The list was compiled just prior to publication of the present volume; the information provided here may change. Be aware that many organizations take several weeks or longer to respond to inquiries, so allow as much time as possible.

American Friends Service Committee (AFSC)
1501 Cherry Street, Philadelphia, PA   19102
(800) 345-4712
Web site: www.afsc.org

The American Friends Service Committee (AFSC) carries out service, development, social justice, and peace programs throughout the world. Founded by Quakers in 1917 to provide conscientious objectors with an opportunity to aid civilian war victims, AFSC attracts the support and partnership of people of many races, religions, and cultures.

American Legion
National Headquarters, Indianapolis Office
Indianapolis, IN   46206
(317) 630-1200 • fax (317) 734-8671
Web site: www.legion.org

The American Legion was chartered by Congress in 1919 as a patriotic, wartime veteran's organization. A community-service organization, the legion now numbers nearly 3 million members—men and women—in nearly fifteen thousand American Legion Posts worldwide.

Center on Conscience and War (CCW)
1830 Connecticut NW, Washington, DC   20009

(202) 483-2220 • fax: (202) 483-1246
e-mail: ccw@centeronscience.org
Web site: www.centeronconscience.org

The Center on Conscience and War (CCW), formerly the National Interreligious Service Board for Conscientious Objectors (NISBCO), was formed in 1940 by an association of religious bodies. CCW works to defend and extend the rights of conscientious objectors. The center is committed to supporting all those who question participation in war, whether they are U.S. citizens, permanent residents, documented or undocumented immigrants—or citizens in other countries.

Courage to Refuse
Refuser Solidarity Network
PO Box 5374
Washington, DC   20009
(202) 232-1100
Web site: www.seruv.org/english

Courage to Refuse is a movement that grew out of the Combatants Letter—a letter which was first published on January 2002 and has since been signed by hundreds of combat reserve soldiers in the Israel Defense Forces (IDF). The signers believe the activities of the IDF have nothing to do with the defense of the State of Israel, but are rather intended to expand the colonies at the price of oppressing the local Palestinian population. Over 280 of the signers served prison terms for their refusal to serve in the occupied territories.

Mothers Against the Draft
186 Ryndon, Unit 12, Elko, NV   89801
(775) 753-6397
Web site: www.mothersagainstthedraft.org

Mothers Against the Draft was founded by a group of concerned mothers and grandmothers united in opposition to reinstituting a military draft or any other form of compulsory national services. The organization distributes the newsletter *MAD News Journal* free via e-mail.

Quaker Council for European Affairs (QCEA)

Square Ambiorix 50, Brussels   1000
  Belgium
(32) 2230 49 35 • fax: (32) 2230 63 70
e-mail: info@qcea.org
Web site: www.quaker.org/qcea

The Quaker Council for European Affairs (QCEA) was founded in 1979 to promote the values of the Religious Society of Friends (Quakers) in the European context. QCEA works to express a Quaker vision in matters of peace, human rights, and economic justice. Among the human rights issues it is concerned with are conscription and conscientious objection.

U.S. Selective Service

Public and Intergovernmental Affairs
Arlington, VA   22209-2425
(703) 605-4100 • fax: (703) 605-4106
e-mail: information@sss.gov
Web site: www.sss.gov

The Selective Service System is an independent federal agency operating with permanent authorization under the Military Selective Service Act. It is not part of the Department of Defense; however, it exists to serve the emergency manpower needs of the military by conscripting untrained manpower, or personnel with professional health-care skills, if directed by Congress and the president in a national crisis. Its statutory missions also include being ready to administer an alternative service program in lieu of military service, for men classified as conscientious objectors.

Veterans of Foreign Wars (VFW)

406 West thirtieth Street, Kansas City, MO   64111
(816) 756-3390
Web site: www.vfw.org

The Veterans of Foreign Wars (VFW) is active in community-service programs and special projects. From providing free phone cards to the nation's active-duty military personnel to raising money for the World War II memorial the VFW works to fulfill its mission of "honoring the dead by helping the living."

Vietnam Veterans of America (VVA)
8605 Cameron Street, Suite 400, Silver Spring, MD   20910
(301) 585-4000 • fax: (301) 585-0519
Web site: www.vva.org

Founded in 1978, the Vietnam Veterans of America (VVA) is the only national Vietnam veteran's organization congressionally chartered and exclusively dedicated to Vietnam-era veterans and their families.

For Further Research

Books

Martin Anderson, ed., *The Military Draft: Selected Readings on Conscription.* Stanford, CA: Hoover Institution Press, 1982.

———, *Registration and the Draft: Proceedings of the Hoover-Rochester Conference on the All-Volunteer Force.* Stanford, CA: Hoover Institution Press, 1982.

Lawrence M. Baskir and William A. Strauss, *Chance and Circumstance: The Draft, the War, and the Vietnam Generation.* New York: Knopf, 1978.

Iver Bernstein, *The New York City Draft Riots: Their Significance for American Society and Politics in the Age of the Civil War.* New York: Oxford University Press, 1990.

Peter Brock, ed., *"These Strange Criminals": An Anthology of Prison Memoirs by Conscientious Objectors from the Great War to the Cold War.* Toronto: University of Toronto Press, 2004.

Jean Carper, *Bitter Greetings: The Scandal of the Military Draft.* New York: Grossman Publishers, 1967.

J. Garry Clifford, *The Citizen Soldiers: The Plattsburg Training Camp Movement 1913–1920.* Lexington: University Press of Kentucky, 1973.

J. Garry Clifford and Samuel R. Spencer Jr., *The First Peacetime Draft.* Lawrence: University Press of Kansas, 1986.

Eliot A. Cohen, *Citizens and Soldiers: The Dilemma of Military Service.* Ithaca, NY: Cornell University Press, 1985.

Richard Danzig and Peter Szanton, *National Service: What Would It Mean?* Lexington, MA: Lexington Books/DC Heath, 1986.

George Q. Flynn, *The Draft: 1940–1973*. Lawrence: University Press of Kansas, 1993.

———, *Conscription and Democracy: The Draft in France, Britain, and the U.S.* Westport, CT: Greenwood Press, 2002.

Ute Frevert, *A Nation in Barracks: Modern Germany, Military Conscription, and Civil Society*, trans. Andrew Borcham with Daniel Brueckenhaus. Oxford, UK: Berg, 2004.

Philip Gold, *The Coming Draft*. New York: Ballantine Books, 2006.

Tom Hickman, *The Call-Up: A History of National Service*. London: Headline Book Publishing, 2004.

Peretz Kidron, ed., *Refusenik! Israel's Soldiers of Conscience*. London: Zed Books, 2004.

Stephen M. Kohn, *Jailed for Peace: The History of American Draft Law Violators, 1685–1985*. Westport, CT: Greenwood Press, 1986.

James C. Miller III, ed., *Why the Draft? The Case for a Volunteer Army*. Baltimore, MD: Penguin, 1968.

Daniel Moran and Arthur Waldron, eds., *The People in Arms: Military Myth and National Mobilization Since the French Revolution*. Cambridge: Cambridge University Press, 2003.

J.K. Osborne, *I Refuse*. Philadelphia: Westminster Press, 1971.

John O'Sullivan and Alan M. Meckler, eds., *The Draft and Its Enemies: A Documentary History*. Urbana: University of Illinois Press, 1974.

Barnet Schechter, *The Devil's Own Work: The Civil War Draft Riots and the Fight to Reconstruct America*. New York: Walker and Company, 2005.

Sol Tax, ed., *The Draft: A Handbook of Facts and Alternatives*. Chicago: University of Chicago Press, 1967.

John Whiteclay Chambers II, *To Raise an Army: The Draft Comes to Modern America*. New York: Free Press, 1987.

Internet Sources

Jim Carey, "Bring Back the Draft . . . NOT," *Military.com*, April 26, 2004. www.military.com.

David Hackworth, "Uncle Sam Will Soon Want Your Kids," *Military.com*, October 4, 2004. www.military.com.

Stanley Kober, "To Reduce Military Tensions in Europe, Ban Conscription," Cato Institute, March 19, 1989. www.cato.org.

Catherine Miller, "The Death of Conscription," BBC News, June 29, 2001. http://news.bbc.co.uk.

Tony Paterson, "Schroder to End Conscription in Push for EU Rapid Reaction Force," *Telegraph.co.uk*, December 4, 2003. www.telegraph.co.uk.

Peter Shapiro, ed., "The Citizen Soldier: A History of National Service in America," Center for Political Leadership and Participation, 1994. www.academy.umd.edu/publications/NationalService/citizen_soldier.htm.

Index